Business
by Faith

A Journey of Integrating the Four D's of Success

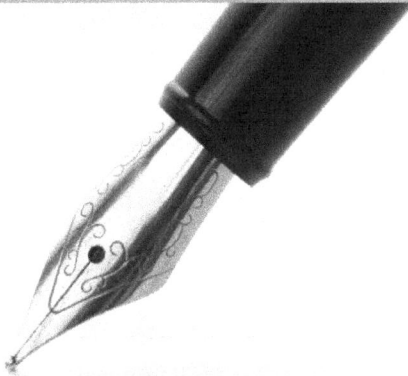

A Modern Day Example
of Unwavering Faith

Linda L. Smith

ZOE LIFE Publications, Inc.

Riverside, CA

Business by Faith © 2015 by Linda L. Smith

Volume I: A Modern Day Example of Unwavering Faith

ISBN 13: 978-1-934556-72-6

Library of Congress Control Number: 2015901717

Published by: **Zoe Life Publications, Inc.**
Post Office Box 310096
Fontana, CA 92331

Editor: Linda L. Smith

Cover Design: Jiong Li and Amanda Johnson

Printed in the United States of America

Dedication

Business by Faith is dedicated to my husband of 34 years, to our daughters, to Brother and Sister Overstreet, and to my father and mother. Each has played a vital role in shaping my life.

To my dearest husband, Ernell, I am thankful for your quiet spirit and unwavering support and love. Thank you for standing by me as I have traveled a road twisted through life, one with many heartaches and tears. I am comforted in knowing you will always be at my side till death parts us.

To my beautiful daughters, Tahira and Aisha, both of you are precious gifts from God. I am blessed to have such beautiful, intelligent, God-loving daughters. Your support, words of encouragement, and love have played an intricate role in my development as a mother and a friend to each of you.

To Brother and Sister Overstreet, whom God sent into my life, thank you for picking me up every Sunday and throughout the week and taking me to church from the tender age of six through the age of seventeen. Thank you for taking me to the house of worship where my love for God and my Spirit was nurtured.

To my Dad, Walter Russ, even though you are physically gone from this earth, your love and spirit lives within me. Oh, how blessed I was to have a father who spent hours on the telephone talking with me about life, the Lord, and His goodness, praying with me through heartaches and tears, believing in me, and encouraging me to be my best as a Christian. Your positive outlook on life and the simplicity of living has afforded me the privilege of being a happier person. Daddy, I found my Peace and I will never lose It!

To my mother, Eula Russ, I thank you for life. Although not unique, my journey has been on a road less traveled by others.

Acknowledgments

Thank you to those students at Four-D College who first asked me to write a book and planted the seed.

To Pastor Tommy and Dr. Gloria Morrow for their love and support. To Dr. Gloria Morrow for applying her professional services as a Clinical Psychologist to help me come out of the darkness, to develop an understanding of life's circumstances, and to find peace therein.

To my dear friend, Donna Bostic, for many years of friendship.

To my wonderful mother-in-law, Vivian Smith, I am thankful to God for putting me into your life.

To the Four-D College family, thank you for 18 years of support and for helping me to make a difference in so many people's lives.

Lastly, to Starla Porter, my Publisher of Zoe Life Publications for asking to read my first journal, and believing *Business by Faith* had to be shared to inspire others.

A Note from Tahira Smith

Desire, determination, drive, and deliverance. Many have dreams of success to be earned; however, few have listened to the Lord's calling to carry out those dreams. Thank you for being an inspiration to me and others as you held steadfast to your mission to serve your community by providing high-quality healthcare education.

As a former student of Four-D College, I had the opportunity to experience your mission of community enrichment through education, and my success fueled a burning desire for higher achievement. The desire for achievement coupled with your often-repeated statement recognizant of early childhood "Always do the best you can and let your reputation precede you" has supported me on the path of success that I once thought was unobtainable. Thank you for your exemplary guidance in my continuing success.

A Note from Aisha Thompson

When meeting with business associates or conducting interviews, I often get asked how I got started working with Four-D College. My response is generally the same. I inform them that Mrs. Smith is my mother and that I began when I was in college as a file clerk, a receptionist, and subsequently in various departments learning the operations of the school. What I don't tell them is of my first non-paying work experience job with Four-D College.

My mother started the school when I was a freshman in high school. When she found her first location, she asked me to help her set it up. We arrived early in the morning, ready to work, I thought I was going to unpack boxes, but she had other plans. She glanced at the bucket on the floor full of cleaning supplies and told me to go clean the restroom. I paused and asked, "Are you serious?" She replied, "Girl, yes, I'm serious! Clean the toilet." I replied, "But…it's a public restroom." She stated, "I don't care, I want it cleaned. I don't want students using a dirty restroom." With a haughty teenager attitude, I said, "Don't they have custodial staff to do that? The other businesses use the restroom too. That's gross." She slowly turned my way, tilted her head down and gave me that dreadful mother stare as if to say, *"Do it now. Do not question me again and make sure you do it right."* Needless to say, the restroom sparkled that morning. Thank you for teaching me that success is achieved through hard work and humility.

A Note from Ernell Smith

Life's journey is forever changing, but the one constant that has always remained the same has been your love and companionship. As of this writing, our marriage has endured 34 years. You are a gift from God and I am truly blessed to be your husband.

You have been an inspiration for all who have come in contact with you. The hearts and souls that you have touched are too numerous to even begin to count. The caring and generosity that comes from you truly comes from your heart.

As I reflect and reminisce on the early years of our marriage, I see in you now the same caring, nurturing person that you were then. Your desire to help and serve remains unchanged. The personal standards that you have established have been enormous. This is evident with our two beautiful daughters who have grown to become outstanding women with great integrity, drive, and character. They truly have followed your lead.

The writing of this book is an accumulation of the trials and tribulations that you have endured throughout the years. Your unwavering faith and your total commitment has been your constant companion all through this journey. Linda, you are a special person and God placed you on earth for a purpose, which you are fulfilling. As you continue your journey I know that you will always remain humble and maintain your desire to be of assistance to those in need.

Lastly, without any doubt, I want you to know this: Just as your faith in the Lord is unwavering, my genuine support in what you do to enhance the lives of others will always be uncompromising.

Table of Contents

Dedication	3
Acknowledgments	5
A Note from Tahira Smith	7
A Note from Aisha Thompson	7
A Note from Ernell Smith	8
Foreword	13
Prologue	17
Introduction	19
Journal 1	25
Looking Back …	95
Journal 2	99
Looking Back …	189
Journal 3	193
Looking Back …	271
About the Author	275

Linda L. Smith

Foreword

By Starla Porter

It was about 20 years ago when I first laid eyes on her. I was a recent transplant from the metropolitan Los Angeles area, looking to land on my feet in the Inland Empire. I was browsing through a local newspaper and I vividly remember seeing her face and instantly saying to myself, "Wow, *she's a beautiful Black woman!"* Little did I know 20 years later, she and I would become business acquaintances and that relationship would evolve into a friendship of sisterhood that will certainly last a lifetime.

I grew up in South Central Los Angeles and women of substance, successful business women to be exact, were scarce. I looked for what I called 'sheroes' and would find there were few. So when my path crossed with Linda Lee Smith's, as a result of my company providing printing services for her colleges, it was refreshing to eventually meet someone of her caliber who was not haughty in spirit, but down-to-earth and approachable.

During one of my business visits, I noticed one of her employees was anxious to return to the staff meeting. I had heard about the weekly pep talks with her staff, and I had to ask if these inspirational speeches were being taped. The publisher in me saw an opportunity.

Fast-forward a couple of weeks. I was engaged in a full conversation with this visionary of Four-D College and learned, during our brief but impactful conversation, that she kept a journal nearby and had for many, many years. When I asked her if I could read one, she said she couldn't understand why I would have any interest in her journals. I must admit my motives were purely selfish: I wanted to know what someone like her wrote about every day.

13

About a week later, we met in the parking lot of her campus and she reluctantly relinquished the first journal to me. She had over a dozen at that time, so starting with the first one made sense. I promised to care for it with my life, and that evening I embarked upon a journey that has fascinated me still 'til this day. Unable to put the journal down, I read it in its entirety through the night. I called her and told her and, once again, she could not believe my interest.

Authenticity is a character trait lost in a world of quick, fast, and hurry up about it! Consistency is another behavior quickly losing its luster, as many are too busy trying to keep up with the façades of reality versus real life. Linda Lee Smith is the real deal, no questions asked. She is the embodiment of vision and has measurable results to prove it. She never toots her own horn and really can seem a tad bit naïve about the monumental journey her life unfolds daily.

Quality relationships take work, and this series provides a glimpse into the world of one who is so driven to please her God, that she will not compromise her purpose for any one! On the brink of divorce, best friend woes, death among the living she loved, she still managed to navigate through it all with strong faith, perseverance, hope, and determination to remain unwavering to the call that was placed on her life. Her story is applicable to anyone who endeavors to become a leader within their chosen field of expertise, learning from the one whom reveals all through each page unselfishly.

From business, family matters, relationships, or her faith, she remains true to herself, her calling, and her purpose as defined so effortlessly on the pages of *Business by Faith*. One cannot read these series of books and not be impacted to the core of their being, because her life really has become an open book of discovery to all. There's something within each line and page that will resonate with the reader. Be it struggles with starting up a business, maintaining the business, expanding the business—she has withheld nothing. And it's easy to create a blueprint for success no matter what capacity of leadership or business one may be in.

Destiny has allowed me to call this woman a trusted mentor and friend. Her business savvy has added enormous value to my life and business doings. Having earned a master's degree in business, the lessons I learn from her are not found in a classroom setting but from her business experiences that sometimes plays out like a soap opera. What I have read in her books and have seen with my own eyes keeps me mindful of the resilience required to be true to what I have been called to do in my own life and business. I can successfully live a life of service without compromise personally and professionally by following her example. Simply, I found a 'sheroe' in Linda L. Smith. She is the mentor and leader needed to guide others, as she keeps it pure and honest regarding the woes and victories of business in *Business by Faith*.

Newspaper articles are still highlighting her journey all these years later, allowing me to celebrate her still.

"Iron sharpens iron" is a philosophy that is reciprocated between the two of us in business and in sisterhood. I have no doubts that we both serve one another richly and genuinely. I am equally convinced that every reader will be left to simmer in her words, her journey, and her life—it is full of business nuggets, passion, faith, and love for mankind.

Truly, is there any better way to extend ourselves?

Linda L. Smith

Prologue

On July 31, 1991 at 1:05 a.m., I was called by name. The Lord called me out of a deep sleep, and I said, "Lord it's 1:05 in the morning. Tell me what You want me to know and I will get it in the morning, I'm tired."

And then I thought, *He called me.* How do you explain being called by a voice you don't hear, but you know He is calling you?

"Lord, I'm here, I'm here. I'm coming right now."

I got out of my bed and grabbed a pen and paper. I went into my bathroom, sat down on the throne, and said, "Jesus, I'm here and I'm listening."

And I began to have a conversation with the Lord, and as He spoke to me, I began to write.

The Lord gave me the vision of a school and He told me what to call it. I said, "No Lord, occupation sounds heavy, institution is too large. No, we can't go with college!" I got nervous. I was having palpitations. "What is this? What are these Four-D's?"

And as He spoke to me, I began to write.

"One must have the Desire to achieve. You must have Determination to follow through the process. You must have Drive – that energy level needed to be consistent. And if you do those things, you will have Deliverance, and that's reaching your goals for success."

And I asked the Lord, "Who am I to serve?"

I became overwhelmed by His presence and the conversation we were having. And I said, "Lord, give me something to hold on to," and the Lord gave me Psalms 119:105, *"Thy word is a lamp unto my feet and a light unto my path."* And light my path, He has…

Linda L. Smith

Introduction

When God gives you His word, you know you can always count on it. You can bank on it. His word is better than any man's I know, including my husband's. I trust Him because He has carried me though the most difficult times I could ever imagine. He has been faithful to me just as I have been to Him. I have learned how to trust in His plans for me. What I have done, I don't think is that unusual, not the school. I think what I have done that is unusual is put the degree of the faith I have put in Him.

So often I hear individuals talk about the things they're going to do…that they have been called to do this or that, but they are waiting to see if God is going to call them again. There are people who say, "I know He called me, but I am not ready yet…I have to get my money together, I have to do this and I have to do that, and then I'm going to do it... I have to wait for another sign."

Let me tell you this: When God calls you, you need to move. You need to step out on what you hear Sunday after Sunday, week after week in Bible study where you hear words of belief and faith. You need to put what you hear into action. That's all that I did.

When He called me, I responded. I quit my job. That's how much faith I had. I had a great job as a corporate nurse director with twelve hospitals traveling the country, taking care of patients, and educating nurses. I had access to a company car and credit cards. Yes, when God called me, I quit right away and went to work on the vision He gave me.

My husband thought I was crazy. "What did you do?"

My kids were running around the house asking, "Mommy, are we going to be poor?"

My husband was standing over me with his hands on his hips. I felt like a little child looking up at her father, getting ready to get scolded. At that moment, all I could do was look up at my husband and say, "Jesus."

The battle was over; he couldn't win that one.

There were no words to express or explain my psychological state. *I was called by God.* I expect people to think I was crazy. How many are going to quit their job and go home and say, "Okay Lord, what do I do next?" and wait on the Lord?

I began an indescribable level of journaling and writing. I would pray and ask God to show favor. I prayed for my faith not to waiver one inch as I stayed focused on the plans and purpose He had called me to. God began to put me in places and in front of people and doors that just seemed to open. From writing proposals, to walking into hospital administrative offices and telling them, "Hey, I'm getting ready to open up a school and I need equipment."

They would look at me like I was crazy! I would proceed to tell them what I needed, "I need some beds, I need some tables, I need some linen, give me a couple of sheets."

They would be stunned, but the next thing I knew, I would get a call from the hospital's supply department saying, "You know, I don't know why, but the administrator told us to put you on our account. What is it that you need? We just placed some beds out in the driveway. If you want them, we need for you to come and get them."

Situations like that continued to unfold, and I began to put together what God was orchestrating for me to do. In September of the following year, I started Four-D College with only two students. Someone gave me this scripture and it still hangs in my office. Ephesians 3:20, *"Now unto him that is able to do exceeding abundantly above all that we ask or think, according to the power that worketh in us."*

That power that works in us is faith. God will do abundantly and exceedingly above the power that you have in you. What I am saying is nothing new; we have heard many messages of faith. Faith is truly the power of belief.

Do you believe what you believe, that God is all and all? Do you believe when you say all things are possible? Do you believe that He can heal you when you are sick? Do you believe that He will help you get that job, or present you with that job when you are without one? Do you believe it? That is faith!

The one thing that I have learned and am sure of with Four-D College is the development of my faith. I have been put through so many trials that it's unbelievable, like trials of not having money.

Generally speaking, when you have debt and can't pay your debt, you think about your options, another way out. But when you are thousands of dollars in debt, and you don't see any money before you, you had better develop some faith. I have been there with no money and bills due. Let me tell you about God. When I first started, I was $3,000 in debt. It doesn't matter if you owe $3,000 or $30,000. Been there, done that on both, and it really doesn't matter. I had no money and I was $3,000 in debt. I sat there and said, "Lord, I have no money." So I took my bills and I put them in a folder and I marked these words on it — Bills Due. I got up and said, "Lord, You have some bills to pay. I'll be back." I literally got up and walked out of my office. All that was left were the words, the secretary, and me.

I decided to leave and she said, "Where you going?"

"I don't know where I'm going, but I'll be back."

I came back a few hours later, and as I was getting to the office, I was skipping to the stairs. I was light as a feather. I opened up the door and she was hanging up the phone, looking amazed, "Mrs. Smith, that was Beverly from the city and they want to know if you want a contract with the city for $28,000?"

"What did you tell her?"

"I told her you would call her back."

I immediately called her back and told her yes, we would take the check and we would do the business for that amount. Clearly, that was God working. I had nothing to do with that. It was all orchestrated by the Lord. The $3,000 was covered, and that depth, that same measure of faith is the kind of faith that I need when I have bills that are coming in at $300,000. There is no difference!

It is God's grace that keeps us and we must have faith in Him. It is by faith that I know God and that I strive to have a stronger, deeper relationship with Him. Philippians 3:14 says, "I press toward the goal for the prize of the upward call of God in Christ Jesus." I gave thought to the word 'upward.'

Where is my Heavenly Father when I am positioned and how do I pray? When I look unto the hills that cometh my help, I look upward. I press forward. No matter what's in front of me, I am going to move it, go through it, go around it, and I will be on the other side of it as I press forward to the higher calling of God. As we press forward to the higher calling of God and the purpose of what we are here to do, we should consider the end result of our life. The Word tells us that we should have faith, because it is our faith that will get us into His presence and not our works. We could work all day and not believe.

We have people that come to Four-D and say, "I'm so happy to be here because I couldn't pray where I worked before." It's possible to work hard and take all the credit; that won't get you anywhere in the long run. But when you pray and acknowledge God, He will be in your midst. So I do look upward towards God. I thank Him for my life. I thank Him for the godly character that I have, and the person that I am. I asked the Lord to let my goodness shine, and to maintain a foundation to where I can stand and pray. To help me to always make a difference in someone's life. I truly do believe that I can do all things through Him. I hope that my legacy would be my unwavering faith in God.

My time will come to an end with Four-D College just as my time will come to an end here on earth, but I sincerely hope to be remembered as a person who believed in God. That I had total faith in my Father as He took a small, rejected, and unloved child, and gave me more love than I could handle. That He took this child and stood her upright, and dusted her off because He remembers that day I covered myself in dust and prayed to disappear. Yes, He dusted me off and washed me up. He baptized me, He forgave me of my sins, and He petitioned me to go forth, and I used the foundation given me to pray and make a difference in someone else's life.

My legacy is my faith in God because it is what drives me. I am so grateful to God for the opportunity to say yes to Him, and to be an example of faith for others to glean from. I pray that the stories I have shared resonate and inspire someone to a point of action…

And that, by the end of this book, you know that "Through God, all things are possible."

Who would have thought, that after many years of writing from the depths of my heart, that my private time with the Lord would come to this? Seven journals and many notations later, I give Him praise and honor for always meeting me right where I was. What started as a simple form of relaxation and personal therapy has turned into what I've been told is a fine example of modern day faith. So with all the gratitude that I can muster up at this time, I'm grateful to you, the reader, for taking this journey with me. It hasn't always been pleasant, nor has it been an easy road to pave. However, it has been an extraordinary exploration as I have witnessed the Lord God do more than I could have ever imagined He would through my life.

Without regret, I have made certain that you get a genuine glimpse of my life up close and personal as each entry was written. In chronological order, I share my innermost thoughts and feelings as they pertain to my dreams, faith, family, business, relationships, and intimate concerns. My hope is to provide some insight into the life and times of a woman driven to please her Lord, and purposed since childhood to make a difference in the lives of those she engages.

Within each journal entry shared, I trust you discover traces of hope that will inspire you, courage that will empower you, and faith that will take you places that you have always dreamed of.

Most importantly, may you truly understand how integrating the Four D's of Success as solid principles for successful daily living is applicable to your own journey in life, family, and business…and get to it!

With Love,

Linda Lee Smith

Business by Faith

Journal 1

Begins: August 12, 1991 ~ 10:31 p.m.

Ends: July 29, 1994 ~ 5:10 p.m.

8/12/91 ~ 10:31 p.m.

It's only the second night here and I miss home. Ernell is going camping with some friends, and I know my girls are having a ball in Catalina. This class is very interesting. I'm learning how to adopt my knowledge as a Registered Nurse (RN) and transfer it into the language of an educator. I expect to learn the tools needed to enable me to be an excellent educator. I would have challenged some of the course content if I could have. I like to see what I know. Many times, I surprise myself because I know or understand more than I give myself credit for. I've always been my own toughest critic. I should never underestimate myself.

8/13/91 ~ 4:20 p.m.

I must think this through. How will I incorporate these levels of learning into my classroom? To enhance and increase student learning, I would devise a teaching format that includes more role-playing and acting out situations that involve the students in preparing portions of the lecture, such as giving reports and doing research papers. Time can also be allowed for learning activities in clinical classroom skills. This has been an educational day. I learned new concepts and how to apply them.

8/14/91 ~ 11:45 a.m.

This morning has been a challenge for me. I find myself confused and anxious over the development of the lesson plans, notes, and evaluation tools. I know how to do these things—it's just so much, and it seems overwhelming. I wish the discussions coming on the Feb. and Mar. 1992 assignments could be held off. Application will be my survival. I must not delay in starting my independent studies. Although it's great to be challenged, I keep reflecting on other things I'm held accountable for with my job, personal goals, and family responsibilities. Time management, good time management is a MUST!

10/14/91 ~ 3:15 p.m.

Reflect: What am I going to do differently?

1. To promote class participation, I am going to involve the students on the rule-making process for class conduct.
2. Involve students in the teaching process by seeking out their goals. What do they want to learn? What is their educational objective?
3. Try to provide an "open learning forum" by allowing students to learn at a self-pace with guidance. Hopefully the higher achievers will remain interested and stimulated.

10/15/91

I am learning new concepts and it's funny that I feel anxious. I am thinking about my assignments due, my trip to Houston to work on care plans, and my own personal project. Whoa! I think too broad and too deep. I spend 4-5 hours doing a lesson plan with four points for Susan, instructor at California Polytechnic Pomona, to review. I needed to know I was going in the right DIRECTION. Well, thank goodness it was only a draft. I think Susan will be hearing from me a LOT. I can't wait to get home for a good night of sleep!

10/16/91 ~ 7:35 a.m.

This is it. I made it. I feel good. While sitting here writing at the desk, I get a glimpse of myself in the mirror... I see success!

10/16/91

Entry made on daily evaluation.... This week has been a very positive stimulus for me. I learned new concepts, techniques, and application of theory to enhance my abilities as an educator. Thanks, Ladies!

Sincerely, Linda Smith

I know not where I'm going, but I know my path is set.

8/20/92

It's been a long time since I've picked up this journal. A lot has happened. God is good! I was introduced to Mary Ann Payne by Michelle Daisy in May. Mary assisted with the development of my brochure. She also provided me with information on applying for Job Training partnership Act (JTPA) funds. What a blessing. I had been praying about providing education and training without charging the public.

My first proposal was ACCEPTED by San Bernardino County. I opened my door to the Academy on August 4, 1992. The consultant from Vocational Educational came by on August 12th, and Ms. Luna from Department of Health Services (DHS) called on August 18th. I pray that ALL is final by August 21st.

8/31/92

I feel such despair. My program has been reassigned for the third time to another reviewer and she is out sick today. Lord, guide me, I feel lost. State Fund has not provided me with written notice of coverage for Workers Comp. I've been working on this project since April, early May. I pray that the Lord Jesus will continue to guide and lead me. Open the doors for opportunities to educate, train, and inspire others to do their best. I pray that what I do reflects the best I can do and it is of good Christian character. I envision Four-D Success to be successful. A lamp unto my feet A light unto my path! God, Please Bless this Program.

9/7/92 ~ 12:45 a.m.

Dear Lord, guide me in the right path and keep me focused. I pray that I do not lose sight of the vision. Thank You for the shield of armor. Through Your loving grace, I find security, peace, and love. Thank You for answering my prayer. You made the events leading to my separation from Grand Care happen. I thank You for the thoughts I think and the words I speak. Thank You for my calmness and joy as I sat and listened to the horrible lies being presented by Myra May, for I know that You are my Father in Heaven and that I am covered by the blood of the Lamb.

Thank You, Your Child in Christ Jesus, Linda L. Smith

9/10/92 ~ 5:55 p.m.

"God is Good"

I received the approval from the Department of Health! I am officially and legally a certified Vocational Training School as of September 9, 1992. I am so excited I forgot to make an entry yesterday. I have so many things to do; my mind is ticking so fast in order to prepare for the opening school day of September 14th.

I thanked God yesterday. Overwhelmed with joy, it was difficult to pray. All I could simply say was, "Thank You, Jesus, for the blessings You have bestowed upon me. Use me and keep me focused on the vision. Bless Four-D Success Academy." Tears of Joy!

10/5/92

There are times I feel such despair. I question how am I going to do this and why aren't the students coming? Lord, guide me. Open up the hearts of those who control where the students should be placed. I pray that their hearts soften. I pray for students to start on October 12th, as if this day I have not received any confirmations. Bills are piling up. JTPA has not reimbursed me as of yet, $640.00

My dear friend Michelle Daisy is ill; she was diagnosed with terminal cancer and has been hospitalized. I pray that the Lord lay His healing hand upon her and remove the pain and disease that harbors in her. I pray for her peace of mind, body, and spirit. Lanell's husband's funeral was Friday October 2nd. They were married 26 years. God be with her and her children. I pray for 'good' news tomorrow.

10/9/92 ~ 9:10 a.m.
My cousin David, Pastor Torrence, prayed with me last week. I think it was on Friday the 2nd. He said something good was to happen this week and it did. Larry Widger from the Victorville office came on Tuesday the 6th to assess my program, and he said he was quite pleased, that he would give very positive remarks. I have an appointment with the senior counselor and the Department of Rehabilitation to assess my school. I pray she finds favor in FDSA and me!

The Urban League rep, Tonya Smith came by to assess how Pam is doing and to discuss my reimbursement. The money will surely help. Mary Ann has been a wonderful asset. She wrote a great press release and will have it placed in eight papers. She is allowing 'months' of grace time to pay her for her services.

Curtis input my Logo onto his computer. He too has been wonderful. I owe him so much. He has been kind enough not to tell me how much ☺!

God is good and I must wait on the Lord for He knows my needs and He knows my 'stage of preparation'.

Al and I talked this morning about Michelle. He's in such pain, for he and I know we will not have the opportunity to have her and her bossy ways with us much longer. A part of me knows she is dying, I see how the Cancer has taken its toll. Yet I know that God's will is His own.

Michelle you have been a great friend and sister. I miss you already. I would rather hear you fussing than not! AKA THE GENERAL & RED. We called her The General or Red because, at times, she was so bossy.

10/19/92 ~ 5:15 p.m.

Michelle Blackburn Daisy passed away on October 16th at 9:55 p.m. She was at home with family and friends (me) at her bedside.

As I look back on that hectic day... I rose with intense feelings that I had to make sure Daisy's house was in order for her arrival. I know she would have a fit if it wasn't. After taking my girls to school, I drove directly to her house. I assisted with the laundry, cleaned the kitchen, mopped the floor, made a bed, and had Ty-Ty clean up his room.

I had to go to my office at 10:00 to deal with phone problems. At 12:00, I returned home to dress for my Sorority meeting that evening before going back to Michelle's house. By 1:00 p.m. I was back at the house with Tyrone & Ty-Ty waiting, and waiting, and waiting. Waiting for them to bring her home from the hospital. In the meantime, Ty-Ty became himself, restless and hungry. At 4:00 I took him to Gumbo's for pickup and we talked about his best friend.

Linda L. Smith

I shared with him how his mother and I were friends and the different categories of friendship.

When we returned by 4:30, Michelle was at home. I gave her a partial bed bath and changed her wet linen. Tyrone gave her oral care. It was wonderful to be at my girlfriend's bedside. I wanted to do all that I could to make her comfortable and to show her how much I cared for and loved her. I left for Carson City at 5:00 for my Sorority Meeting and returned at 9:30.

Tyrone greeted me outside. For an instant, I feared bad news. Instead, he told me of how she was mouthing spiritual songs with her family. When I approached her bedside, I knew I could not leave. Her breathing was chain stroking with periods of apnea.

Her radial pulse, barely felt, was weak, thready. Her color was blanche, lips pale, I knew the clinical signs of pending death and I was paralyzed. I was losing my oldest and dearest friend, a friend with whom I had developed a unique friendship and relationship. My friend who did not pass judgment on me. A friend who knew my darkest secrets. A friend who, even through anger and disagreement, would always hold the secrets to her heart. A friend I loved.

It's unbelievable, at times, that she is dead even though I watched her take her last breath. I am saddened and I cry, but in time, the tears will be no more. I will always be saddened over her death but joyful when I think of her and her bossy 'The General' ways.

I know she is spiritually with God. For that, I am joyful. I'll see you one day by the grace of God.

Your Loving Friend, Linda L. Smith

10/19/92 ~ 5:40 p.m.

I continue to seek funding sources and clients for the Certified Nursing Assistant (CNA) program.

I talked to a student today who was told the Colton office was not going to refer students to my program due to cost. And she had been referred to another program.

I have a call to Mr. Keith Lee. I need to know what is going on, awaiting return call. I had to take time for prayer. It helps to soothe the soul, dismiss confusion, and reaffirm faith.

I ask the Lord to guide me, remove walls, open doors, and provide the funding and students. I'll call the city of San Bernardino tomorrow! I pray for their support!

10/23/92 ~ 4:00 p.m.

I thought of Michelle this morning and found myself crying. I remembered the hand holding in silence on Tuesday before she passed away. It was good for me as well as for her. We looked at each other in silence. Words need not be spoken.

Today I held the 1st Advisory Council meeting.

Members present were:

Donna Bostic - Chairperson

Mary Ann Payne

Chuck Braswell

Roxie Barefield

Member absent, Samuel Thorpe

I am very excited. The knowledge of each member is deep and diverse enough to provide Four-D Success the foundation for solid growth. Thanks to each member.

Today's weather has been as ever changing as the emotions I have experienced. The temperature has gone from cold and cloudy, to 81 degrees and sunny, to windy and rainy at 4 p.m. How wonderful is it to be here!

Thank You, God.

Sincerely, Linda

11/5/92 ~ 5:15 p.m.

This has been a busy 'marketing' week for me. As a result of the meeting with the Director of JTPA, Mr. K Lee, I pursued the office manager of the Victorville and Colton office.

Things seem positive. On Tuesday the 3rd, I made a visit to Victorville. After 1½ hours of meetings, discussing the CNA Program, cost and availability of funds, there seems to be hope!

I had the opportunity to show a presentation to the Colton office staff. Questions were asked and answers given.

Today I received a call from Mr. Robert Rochelle that Easton could come into the program. The managers received me and Four-D Success well. I thank God.

Sitting here in silence, I kneel to pray. I thank God for bringing me thus far, I pray that those in control find me and FDSA in favor and support our program. I pray for students. I pray for Ernell's support, that the Lord bless his business so that he may be able to provide financial support to his business, our home, and to FDSA. I pray that Jesus remove the negative influences of Satan from our lives and our home. I give thanks to Him for Pam, her efforts, dedication, and workmanship. I pray for continued blessings which will allow me to do the Lord's work, run my Ed/Training program, to motivate, educate, instill pride, and self-worth in individuals who feel lost and in need of support.

I truly give thanks to God for my blessings. I truly pray for His guidance, support, love, and protection.

Thanks for this day!

11/5/92 ~ 5:30 p.m.

I think of Michelle daily. I miss her truly. I cry occasionally. God be with you,

Love, Linda

11/12/92 ~ 11:50

I came to the conclusion that the support FDSA needed from JTPA in order to keep its doors open was farfetched.

The Department of Rehab denied the application; since FDSA is on the 2nd floor and without an elevator, candidates in wheelchairs can't access our site. Although it was known that wheelchair bound candidates cannot work as a CNA.

I spoke with Debbie from the Ontario JTPA office. She so 'formally' informed me that one student on that day had qualified for training, but she needed remedial training first for 6 months. JTPA/Ontario does not refer students after March. Therefore this client would be sent in the Fall of '93. It finally occurred to me that the state programs/ offices procrastinate to the point of discouragement for participants and contributors. In order to keep my doors open and to provide the training I desire, I needed to revamp my programs and market to the public. Ads were placed in the papers from Orange County to Pasadena. Calls are coming in. Helen Kilgore is moving to Oklahoma in '93. I will seek a replacement.

I pray to continue to walk in the light and stay on the path.

11/13/92 ~ 5:20 p.m.

Well, today Marcia and Barbara finished the training program. It was a joy to issue a Certification of Completion to both of them. I knew they would do well on the State exam.

I've received several calls from people interested in the program. I pray they actually come in and register. I am full of mixed emotions. I have a contract with the JTPA program that is not being honored. The Ontario Superintendent has made it clear to several clients that she will not send them to FDSA.

Lord, I pray, keep my door of education open. Lord, allow the necessary money to come into those in need. Enable clients with a financial blessing. Guide me Lord Jesus.

11/16/92 ~ 5:20 p.m.

What a blessed day! Three students enrolled in the program. What a wonderful joy to receive funds apart from the JTPA program.

I pray that both classes fill to the capacity. Pam and I continue to brainstorm and organize. Donna, thank you for your precious words of wisdom and advice. Keep FDSA in prayer.

Each step I take is in the path set forth by God. I pray that I continue to remain focused on the philosophy, vision, and the path.

I give praise to God for His blessings on this day.

Thank You, Jesus!

11/20/92 ~ 5:15 p.m.

I've received more calls from several interested persons. God willing, next week will be a blessed week for enrollments.

Julie Bollard came by and prayed with me. I'm grateful for her spiritual warfare on behalf of FDSA, and for her friendship and support.

Another student enrolled today and paid. Thank God for this day.

12/3/92 ~ 8:30 p.m.

I am still here. God continues to bless FDSA. Two new students came today. That makes 6 in total... 2 in the day course and 4 in the evening course. I am almost finished with the Home Health Aide Program. I hope it's approved by March '93. I do think of Michelle Daisy, and the heartache is still present. I do miss her. Her family is fine. Tyrone & Ty were over for dinner this past Sunday. Some things never change. They were due over at 3:00, arrived at 7:30. After my kitchen was clean, they came looking for food. The late but great Daisy tradition continues!

God is working through Aisha to capture the soul of Ernell. I thank GOD for a child who is strong in God and is willing to address those things that are not right.

God's Blessing...

12/7/92 ~ 7:05 p.m.

Happy Birthday, Ernell and Tyrone. A message was left on Tyrone's recorder.

Things are going well even though Cynthia did not return to class.

We are covering a lot of ground. Preparation for patient care in the hospital is on schedule.

Although I am tired, I get a boost of energy once class starts. When I lecture and interact with the students, it's nonstop.

I give praise and thanks to God for my many blessings, my husband, children, family, students, and the guidance I receive daily. I give thanks for my good health and my faith in the Lord. I give thanks for knowing Him.

12/31/92

This is my last entry for 1992. Many thoughts are going through my mind as I think on this year's events.

God has been fantastically wonderful. He has given me a blessed life and He's opened new avenues for me to grow.

Four-D Success Academy has had its doors open since August 4, 1992. I have been blessed with staff, furniture, equipment, contracts, and students. Dec. 1st two students passed the CNA test with flying colors. I paid my January '93 rent... what a blessing!

I have been in prayer that God would grant me the opportunity to have "15" students in my February 15, 1993 class. I believe and I have received! I look forward with excitement to my future. I pray to stay in the light of the Lord.

I close out the year with my dearest friend's memory on my mind, and with love for her in my heart. Michelle Blackburn Daisy, God loves you. He has given me joy and peace. I will never forget you and will always keep you near me.

This evening, close friends are coming over for gumbo. The Ballard's Donna, Cari, Benki, Curtis, Gail and children, Tyrone, and Ty-Ty.

God has given us another day to grow closer to Him. Thank You, Lord.

1993 will be very productive and positive, God-filled, and blessed year for me! STAY HAPPY!!

1/15/93 ~ 6:00 p.m.

I received a call on January 11, 1993 from Colton JTPA asking if I could train a class size of eight for $27,000.00. My Lord, two minutes prior I was asking how would I get through February. How can I market my newly approved Home Health Aide program (HHA)? Well, He answered me! I am preparing to offer the HHA Program. I pray for its success.

I met with Pastor Chuck on 1/12/93 to share FDSA, the goals, and to pray. There is much to do, I continue to pray for wisdom, focus, and strength, to do that which I have been given vision.

Jesus, thank You. As doors open, allow me to step through as the representative You wish me to be.

Again thanks, Your Child in Christ, Linda...

Michelle, Girl God is Good! Love ya! ☺

1/27/93 ~ 7:45 p.m.

It is amazing how much Satan is working against my faith. The Lord has opened doors yet ill thoughts enter into my mind. Will I be able to pay for my bills? Will I receive a contract? The Lord has opened my door and has made a financial way since I received my business license in March '92 and the Lord has NOT brought me this far for me to fail!

I give thanks to His presence in my life, for the people who work with me, those that I owe money to, and those who have provided guidance.

I rebuke Satan in the name of the Lord Jesus Christ, the Almighty. I cast him out of the walls of FDSA, out of my mind, and away from all that is good. Guide me, Lord.

2/4/93 ~ 3:30 p.m.

Well, I am down to $165 and some change in my checking account. But I am not worried. The Lord will provide.

I attended my first Southern California Rehabilitation Exchange (SCRE) meeting, passed out brochures, and met a few people. I pray for positive results. I have begun to interview for my upcoming class.

I am seeking 8 youth. Things come up and I address them as quickly as possible.

I obtained my Contract with Care Home Health. This is great!

I am tired, but I shall go on.

Tomorrow is the 2nd Advisory Committee Meeting.

Have a blessed day.

2/13/93 ~ 3 p.m.

I am still here!

Colton JTPA asked if I would hold a class in San Bernardino for 10-12 adults. Yes of course. I immediately sought out a full-time instructor. On Saturday, the 6th, Adenia inquired about full-time work, and on the 8th, I was offering her a full-time job... Oh, I still don't have any money per se... but I am here. I'm still standing!

I talked with Ernell about finances. He truly is my financial supporter. I owe him thousands. Honey, thanks for believing in me.

I received a call from the West San Gabriel Valley Consortium. They liked my proposal. I am going to be placed on the vendor's list for the 1993 to 1994 year. God is good.

My body is physically tired, my mind does not want to think for a few minutes. I pray for strength and the ability to continue to address issues, to maintain my focus and awareness.

I give my heart to my work. I help others to see their potential. I encourage others to continue upwards. I seek to provide opportunities for economic growth, to increase knowledge. I seek to be of service to another. I love what I do and I thank God for allowing me to help in a manner that is effective, consistent, and truly heartfelt. I have six, yes, six students in my first Home Health Aide Class. This is fun. I am exhausted, but having a ball. Yes, a ball!

2/27/93 ~ 4:06 p.m.

Today, my first Home Health Aide class graduated. All six of them. What a joyful blessing. I thank God that I am able to help others. I pray for continued ability to aid others, to grow and to keep the dream of Four-D Success Academy opened. Thank You, Lord, for this day, a gift of love.

3/3/93 ~ 6:10 p.m.

Thank You, Lord, for the financial blessing. Carlton at JTPA will be advancing an estimated costs need for $9,000, and my intake from the Home Health Aide and private payers enabled me to pay rent, Pam, bills, and buy books.

I'm trying to plan for the future. Will my 1993 to 1994 contract be enough to employ a fulltime instructor? Will I receive additional money for support from other agencies?

A couple of my students have been in need of counseling. One thinks she is pregnant, the other is fearful of not being accepted by JTPA. My goal is to be of assistance. I listened to the first student who is pregnant and recommended she discuss the circumstances with her boyfriend, and or the support person in her family, and to look at all of the support systems that are around her. The second student was denied by JTPA, but her desire is strong and she needs support and an opportunity to grow. She will remain in school at no cost. I know the Lord is blessing me. He guides me daily down an unknown path.

I pray to stay focused, sincere to the cause and prayerful to God. I am so thankful. Amen.

6:35 p.m.

I sit here reading passages. Thoughts of Michelle cross my mind. I smile. Oh how I miss her.

3/10/93 ~ 5:06 p.m.

Yesterday, oh what a blessing! Adenia Williams and I obtained our contract to use Pacific Park Convalescent Hospital in San Bernardino as our clinical site. I showed Adenia the school site and she was pleased. A few things to iron out but all is well.

At the Colton JTPA office, to our surprise, there were 21 clients seeking enrollment. Six had already qualified. I asked Robert what my limit was and he said as many as you feel comfortable with. We could handle 20-25 students. My God... seek and pray, and He answers!

Things are going well in class. The students are learning a lot and anticipate their second test. I will be advertising for my April Home Health Aide class on Friday. God bless this program with success. I see how I am helping others and it feels wonderful. I may not be able to assist everyone, for there are people who refuse to be helped or deny the depressed state they are in. But those that will allow me to assist them, I surely will do my best.

Thank You, Lord, keep me focused and in the path of light. Your Child, Linda

Oh yes, by the way, my second Home Health Aide class has 17 students. Class started March 6th and ended on March 27th.

Linda L. Smith

4/4/93 ~ 12:45 p.m.

I have been in prayer all this week. I pray daily, but my special prayer is to receive a blessing for Four-D Success Academy. I asked the Lord to grant me the wisdom I need to write the upcoming proposal. I pray that He controls the thoughts I think and the words I speak. I pray for a positive spiritual relationship with those I work with and that He guides me to people of God who will find favor in me and my efforts.

On April 2, 1993 I attended a career fair at Norton Air Force Base. Before I got on the freeway I began to pray that the board opens up doors that enable me to meet with the members of the 16th St. Seventh - Day Adventist Church. Lo and behold His goodness. Too excited to write. He sat me next to Martin L. Howard, Interim minister at the 16th St. Seventh-day Adventist Church. All I can say is "Thank You, Jesus." My heart is filled with gratitude and tears flood me. I am so grateful for God's blessings and goodness. It is an honor to help others and it is a blessing to be a child of the Almighty God. Thank You, Jesus.

4/17/93 ~ 4:45 p.m.

April 14th was an emotionally horrible day. I cried and sobbed over the thought of the staff questioning the pay schedule. Payday is the 15th and 30th of each month and Edina had a valid point. Some pay periods were 11 or 12 days and others were 9 and 10 days. Even though staff was paid every two weeks.

I felt, here I am struggling to make ends meet, working endless hours. I have taken home $2,000 in seven months to make sure my bills and staff are paid on time. I felt as though I had given my all only to hear this. I worked without pay to pay her (them).

Ernell took me to lunch and asked, "What can I do to help?" That was all I needed to give me strength and encourage me to continue. Having my man's support and God's guidance, I needed nothing else. Tomorrow is a new day.

I'd met with Ms. Z at Bradbury Manor Duarte. Things will possibly work out if the Lord's willing. Such a lovely place with space to teach and to set up an office. I will hire a part-time registered nurse to work the area. The Foothill proposal looks good. Thank God for this and every day.

Guide me. Keep me focused. There is so much to do. Possible contract with Home Health Agencies. Wow! A silent prayer to the Lord. Amen.

4/20/93 ~ 5:20 p.m.

The Lord is good. He has enabled FDSA to stay open and grow. Somehow, I have hired an accountant full-time and I wait for a registered nurse full-time. I will also seek a placement specialist. Now, I know I have no money, but I know the Lord does and He is plentiful. He has and will continue to provide for Four-D Success Academy needs.

God be with those who have passed and gone home. Today William Brown, choir director, was laid to rest. Michelle, I miss you!

4/23/93 ~ 6:15 a.m.

Jesus, thank You for this day. San Antonio Home Health will sign the contract for students. I have an appointment with the Visiting Nurse Association management next week, and Bradbury Oaks in Duarte will sign a contract for office space in training. What a blessing that things are coming together. The potential contract with

San Bernardino County is for $304,000. I pray I have the opportunity to provide the education and training proposed. Curtis, my accountant, is hanging tight. I feel safe and trust him. I pray God will keep him and the other staff members on one accord. The Lord is good.

Today, Brother Robert L. Elston was laid to rest. God be with his family.

5/2/93 ~ 12:10 p.m.

I dreamed I stepped onto a scale and it registered 991 pounds. I said, "What, 991... maybe the numbers are wrong, maybe I weighed 191 pounds." I should weigh 134 pounds, 150 pounds, but not 191 pounds. I looked at myself, I didn't look like I weighed 191 pounds, and I know I have not been eating right. This scale flashed 991. The face of the scale illuminated with a green message like those in the bank ... news flash!

When I woke up, I told Ernell I had to buy a scale. My dream was a message to lose weight. I saw Perry at Church today and shared my dream. He looked at me and said, "The message is that your proposal will be $991,000—that's the message."

Lord, whatever the message is, I pray I continue to walk in the light of the lamp. Thank You for Your blessings and guidance. Thank You for the path You have set and the doors You have opened. I pray for a new location in Claremont on Foothill to house a growing business. I pray for Christian workers to come to my door to meet the needs of Four-D Success Academy. I pray for three registered nurses, two placement specialists, and a clerk at whatever I need to succeed. Thanks be to Almighty God.

5/11/93~ 5:50 p.m.

Sometimes a blessing comes in an unexpected way. My focus today was on obtaining contracts for funding. I submitted my proposal to San Bernardino (Norton). I met with the Director of Nurses at Casa Colina. Possible contract to train CNA, 23 persons. All this is well and good.

At 4:50 p.m. or so, I received a call from a young lady who began to share her personal problems such as divorce, loss of home, and child, poor legal representation, and her desire to go to school. Her previous low self-esteem had taken a change for the better through communication and education. Her husband feared her growth. As she spoke, I began to realize I was doing the best I could. I listened. I listened for 50 minutes.

Before we departed on the phone, I shared with her God's blessings, Psalms 119:105, and that God would take care of all things in His own time. Fear not, stay on the path of the light. She is an approved cosmetologist. I told her about openings at Nailologist and gave her the phone number. I recommended she seek out Los Angeles Trade Tech LVN program, that she not fear Math and not set limitations in her mind.

My blessing today was that I was able to help another. I thank God for patience, caring, love, and Four-D Success Academy. I was blessed today. God be with you Pat C. in all that you do. He will allow you to rise above all obstacles. Keep your faith in Him.

5/13/93 ~ 3:10 p.m.

Mr. Perkins called today; I got the contract to train displaced workers from Norton Air Force Base! I feel that come July, the doors are going to flood. I pray to be prepared!

Linda L. Smith

I met with the Director of Nurses at Casa Colina this week (May 11, 1993) to discuss the contract to train 23 nursing assistants. God's blessing, it's mine!

Yesterday, 18 students graduated from the San Bernardino class. What a joy. The students were visited by case managers Robert and Edna, from the JTPA office in Colton. Adenia, thank you. God, thank You.

5/19/93 ~ 6:13 p.m.

I submitted my contract proposal to Casa Colina, Friday I will know if it is Four-D Success Academy's or not. I pray for great news.

My account is low and I can't make payroll, but the Lord can! The Red Cross accepted FDSA check for $1,530 and will hold it until June 7, 1993. Lord, the students can test on May 26, 1993. Adenia will let me pay her a week late. God, how He works miracles.

Curtis has set up my financial office in house. Things are going to work out well.

Dear Lord, I pray for FDSA's success. I pray for guidance. I pray to stay focused on goals, and Your word. I ask for forgiveness for my ill behavior with my child, Aisha. I pray for peace, control, and understanding. I pray for a continued loving family (home), my husband and children.

Guide me to be my best. I pray for success, for in it I will be of benefit to others.

Respectfully, Linda

5/20/93 ~ 4:10 p.m.

Jesus, thank You.

I received my approval from my post secondary for all three components, CNA, HHA, and Acute Aide Training (AAT). What a blessing. I developed the brochure a year ago and today it's real.

I received my agreement from Bradbury today.

Meeting today with Chris and Curtis. Good information on becoming a corporation. Lord, bless FDSA with the Casa Colina contract.

5/28/93 ~ 2:10 p.m.

Out of the 18 students who graduated, six failed the skills component. All were in one group. I pray that this never happens again. I know I have little control over the ultimate outcome. But I will always insist that we, as instructors, focus on the learning process of each student. True assessment of their skills is a must.

Lord, guide me. Enable me to be the best I am capable of being.

I pray that I receive the contract vouchers that I seek from all of the proposals submitted. I pray for success with the referral programs, rehab and private.

Carry me, Lord, throughout the upcoming months. Bless FDSA financially. Enable me to hire the staff I need to increase the quality of our performance. In Jesus name, I ask for these things. Amen.

6/1/93 ~ 3:15 p.m.

The account is low. I will need approximately $6,000 to clear bills. Lord, I am borrowing money from the petty cash to get through the day. Worrying doesn't help. Prayer and faith does. I know the Lord will take care of my needs.

As I write, I believe and relax in knowing the goodness and the power of the Lord.

I hope Tahira will enjoy the upcoming trip to see all the colleges between July 9th through the 27th.

Lord, Walter and Jeannie announced their engagement to Ernell and me. They want the wedding and reception held at our house on August 28, 1993.

It is good to know the Lord, for in times like these, He carries me.

6/3/93

Last night, I cried out to the Lord for help. I feel such despair, never have I wanted to give and could not. I have over $6,000 in bills for this month. Dollars are coming slow. Lord, make a way.

I received bad news. The Foothill Consortium and the Los Angeles County denied my proposals. I am unsure actually why the proposals were denied. But an official letter is coming. East San Gabriel is not excepting new vendors.

I must talk with Ernell about options. Where do I go from here? Lord, where do I go from here?

6/5/93 ~ 3:45 p.m.

I received a call on June 3, 1993 at about 4:45 p.m. from Pastor Julius West. He called to inform me he was making contact with members in his region and wanted to see me and pray for any needs or concerns that I may have. Lord, I do need spiritual support and prayer. An appointment was made and Pastor West arrived at my home by 7 p.m. for prayer. It was a true blessing. My husband participated. I think the Lord was sending Pastor West for his support and renewing my strength.

On June 4th, I was told by Steve C. and Joel H. that my proposals were denied. I felt lighthearted. The news did not make me panic. I simply thought how nice to be calm in the face of the enemy. Lord what do I do, where do I go from here? I believe, therefore I shall receive.

At 10 p.m. dressed for bed, I was compelled or spiritually told to write a response to the Foothill Consortium and send it to the Executive Director. After meeting with Jane S., she advised me to send a copy to all the members of the PIC. The letter was mailed and I will appeal to the Board.

This Monday I must meet with Cynthia at the Red Cross to explain FDSA's financial status. JTPA has not mailed the monthly check. Therefore I cannot pay bills!

The Lord will open the door. I must also meet with Casa Colina. Lord, bless this meeting. Let them find favor in the nursing program and me. Bless me with a contract!

6/7/93 ~ 5:45 p.m.

Last night at 8 p.m., I was baking, for the first or second time in my life, a peach cobbler. I was strongly compelled to stop and call Elizabeth Duncan for advice and support.

I dressed and went to my office and called her at home. She advised me to submit a letter to Mr. Kessler and to Mr. Huey as soon as possible and fax it.

I wrote a letter and faxed it out this morning.

This has been a blessed day.

1. One, the Red Cross director will hold the $1,530 check until I tell her to deposit it.
2. JTPA will cut a check for $2,560 within five days. This will help tremendously. $15,000 is coming in July.
3. The telephone company gave me a reprieve until the 14th to pay partial the amount of the $315. The balance is due July 16th.
4. Four, the late rent can be paid by the 10th and will not be deposited until the 16th!
5. I delivered two more proposals. I had the opportunity to meet with Don (Mid-Valley), Garcia (Review) and Ms. Doolittle of Southeast Area Social Service Funding Authority (SASSFA).
6. I met with the CEO of Casa Colina, Linda Montgomery the Director of Nurses (DON) and Candy, the assistant, to discuss the contract. I am awaiting the outcome.
7. I received a call from the rehab program DMS in Diamond Bar. They are interested in placing students at FDSA. They will be here on 6/10 for a facility review.
8. I will be able to enroll in to the Long Beach State credential program for fall. I will meet the 2/1/94 deadline for completion.

9. Contact was made with Mr. Willie White, City Councilman with Pomona. I will seek a letter of support to train Pomona residents.

Lord, thank You for the many blessings. I stand firm in faith. He that is within me is greater than he that is in the world. Thank You, Jesus.

6/8/93 ~ 6:55 p.m.

Met with Nancy Sedlack, previous owner of Health Careers. An excellent resource with good ideas on expansion. She is very encouraging and supportive. We discussed the Small Business Administration (SBA) loan, new programs, the possible use of her building, implementation of rehab training programs for San Bernardino Community Hospital.

Lord, keep Your hands on top and beneath me! I pray that I have success with my appeals.

6/11/93 ~ 3:35 p.m.

A busy week is coming to an end. I take time to reflect on the goodness of the Lord. Deckert okayed half the payment for this month.

Last Friday, I owed $5,000 or more in debt, I had $400 in my account. Today I have $1,600 in my account and I still owe $5,000. The Lord does miracles.

Barbara Dent and Pete West offered letters of support for the Los Angeles appeal. Joe Picken, and Tina H. offered letters of support for the Foothill Consortium. I am still waiting for Casa Colina's decision.

Seeking RN instructors. Met Cynthia Marlatte, Rehab counselor and possible positive connection and referral. Nice person.

Thank You, Lord.

6/16/93 ~ 4:25 p.m.

I appealed the Foothill Consortium and was once again denied. I was told I made a good presentation.

The state needs to receive more paper and make a visit to approve Duarte and S.B. site. Lord, get me through this! I am aiming to hold class in July.

Casa Colina is on hold until? The Chief Operator is ready to sign, but the CEO is having difficulty with the amount of the contract.

The Lord has blessed me financially. I have been able to pay bills (somehow) without the checks bouncing.

Robert says I have $16,000 coming and I project another $16,000-$17,000 in July payment. I pray to manage my finances better and correctly to sustain us through the year-end.

I called Pastor J. West to report this week's outcome. He was unavailable (wife in the hospital). I will pray for her good health.

6/16/93

I received a call today to pick up my much-needed check of more than $16,000. Thank You, Lord.

I sit here thinking about my dear friend Michelle. Oh how I miss her. All that she worked for is lost within eight months after her death. I pray for Tyrone and Ty-Ty. I pray Tyrone will be moved to seek employment and care for his son, relinquish the ways of the world. Michelle truly was the driving force, and the force is gone.

My dear friend, Donna, has offered to take me on a vacation to a place of my choice. Jamaica. What a jewel.

Lady, thanks for your support.

I will always do my best!

6/23/93 ~ 5:28 p.m.

Well, LA County denied my proposal. I will appeal. I spoke with C. Williams about satellites. Hopefully, I will be able to obtain approvals without additional dollars. I asked Nancy Sedlack to put in a good word with the City of San Bernardino (SB) for me.

I am very anxious. It is such a sick feeling to be denied the opportunity to help others when I feel I truly have something good to give and share.

Lord, keep me focused.

6/24/93 ~ 5:15 p.m.

I called Steve Chase with Foothill Consortium. He said he forgot to call me to inform me of the appeal outcome, huh? I was denied, but was placed high on the secondary list. He requested some paperwork. More work with no outcome. I sit here and wonder in amazement the recent denial I received. I wonder of those who were funded wholeheartedly want to give as I do. I don't doubt their sincerity, I just wonder. I know I must develop new avenues of financial support. I will continue to follow leads, submit letters, network, pray. Where do I go from here? UP, UP, UP!

6/28/93 ~ 6:05 p.m.

A bit of good news. SB County approved my contract. Now I must work on getting students. I set an appointment to appeal with LA county for July 1, 1993 at 1:00 p.m. I have appointments with supervisors of the Ontario and Colton Office. Hopefully to set up orientation groups.

I pray that the council and Dept. of Health Services will have my approvals by July 9, 1993.

7/6/93 ~ 9:00 a.m.

I awaken with intense memories of a dream. A dream that told me I would violate God's law of obedience unless I fasted and prayed. I arose at 7:30 a.m. on July 5th and descended to my living room with my Bible. I read every passage pertaining to fasting. I never knew how to prepare for a fast and what it actually meant. As I read, I obtained peace and assurance that this is what I needed and must do to be obedient to the word of God, and I affirm my faith to establish a stronger spiritual relationship with Him. After I read all passages, I rose and, as Matthew 6:17-18 is written, I anointed my head and washed my face and prayed for guidance, strength, wisdom and righteousness.

I happily went through the day not interested in food. I consumed water and juice. I feel great. I give thanks to the Heavenly Father for His love and for choosing me to do this work. I pray I don't disappoint Him.

I met with Ms. Woods today and I pray she finds favor in the school this year. Last year, I only received one student from her office. I pray for many more.

A group of us are planning a fundraiser for Michelle's headstone, and an old fashion picnic will be held on August 25th. We will have a great turnout. God be with you Michelle. Love and miss you!

Linda

7/20/93 ~ 4:58 p.m.

It's been a while since I made an entry. I've been busy trying to coordinate a class for residents who live in SB City/County. This is so stressful, but I dismiss it because I know the Lord is guiding me. I stand at the door and He will open it!

A group of friends are planning a Memorial picnic for Michelle to raise funds for her headstone, and to establish a trust for Ty-Ty. She surely is missed. The picnic is scheduled for July 25th. We expect 100 people. I think many more will show up.

Tahira is having a good time touring, shopping, having freedom! I truly miss my baby. Aisha is running Cross Country. She is enjoying this. I pray for her success in whatever she chooses to do.

Jesus, thank You for this day. Enlighten me, guide me, and protect me.

8/6/93

The picnic for Michelle went well. We collected $300 plus. It was good seeing old friends. Things are going well. I still have the key to the office. I am trying to correlate services between the City and County offices to get going with the CNA Class. It is unbelievable how stressful and confusing this is. I am focusing on Home Health Training. I think that this will be my main support. I pray for favor to open, contracts to be made, in order to do business. I pray I have not strayed from the path. My vision is clear. I pray my walk is straight. I am grateful to God Almighty for the opportunity and privilege He has given me.

Lord, send students for the HHA Class and allow me to open up in SB, Corona, Duarte, Pasadena, and Claremont. I pray each site becomes self-incorporated. I am at a standstill. I feel like I am racing, yet not moving.

8/12/93 ~ 3:50 p.m.

This has been a blessed week. I have been filled with the love of God and joy, joy, joy. Sometimes we need to give thanks for what we have, what we have survived and overcome, and for where we are going. On Tuesday, I had an appointment with SB City to discuss FDSA's program. Staff was not aware of the presentation. but the Lord has a way of working things out. I felt down, not knowing what to expect from the City as far as receiving students. I visited Glenda at the City Recreation Department. She is funny. She has a good listening ear and is intuitive. She detected my pain and inquired, "Girl what's going on? Tell me something." I asked for prayer and I asked for a financial blessing. When all was said and done, I had received a blessing from Glenda, a $165 rental fee, and booked space through December.

Today I met with Nancy Sedlack. There is a possibility that her facility in San Bernardino will be available for rental space. I will pray on it and ask the Lord for guidance.

Vacation is near, August 14th-23rd ... a whole week off. I am nervous about my office operations, things running smoothly. But I must go.

I prayed and shared with the staff yesterday morning about the joy of God in my life, my focus, and my desires for the school. The love of God and His presence in my life is wonderful. There is nothing I cannot do.

I pray for those who are afflicted with disease and pain. I pray for those who do not know the Lord and are missing out on a joyful life. I pray for my salvation.

No HHA class was held this week, as only one student showed up. Next week will be better!

Heavenly Father, I thank You for the guidance You have given me. The contracts, contacts, and financial support. I know through You all things are possible. I pray to stay on the path of righteousness. I pray to stay focused in my journey, to help others and to share the word of God with others. I give You praise, honor, and glory. I thank You for selecting me to do this thing. I pray for a Christian staff that know You and love You.

I pray for financial success, which will enable me to help so many others. Lord, I know You will provide all of my needs. I know Satan will try to cloud my mind. I cast Satan out of my mind, my home, my school, out of the hearts of those I know and do not know, out of the minds of those I missed... Satan, get thee behind my Lord! You have no hold on me, my family, my school, my staff, or anyone I come in contact with.

My God is a powerful God. His power exceeds all that I know and could ever imagine. He guides me, carries me, loves and protects me.

Lord, You know my needs, and the path is laid. I pray to walk it right!

Your Child, Linda

8/23/93 ~ 4:35 p.m.

Back from vacation. Had a wonderful time with family and friends. Willow Beach is so peaceful and relaxing. Ernell and I talked about relocating to Arizona in 10 years. The kids will be long gone, our home will be paid off and we will be ready to go. This has been a slow day. I sit here thinking what I need to do to generate business … several calls made awaiting responses. I seek a jack of all trade marketing, job development person. Emotions are low. There are eight students in this week's class. I pray for full classes at the three sites.

Thank You, Lord for a safe trip. Thank You for FDSA.

9/1/93 ~ 9:25 a.m.

I've been thinking about writing here for several days. Trying to get the SB CNA going. Still waiting for signatures on the contract. County has referred 2 students. Ontario continues to be non-committal. I have scheduled an appointment with Keith Lee. State continues to give confusing information. I have approval to operate, and yet I am being told the SB site is not approved. I am working with my 3rd consultant in 3 months.

Walter and Jeanie got married August 28, 1993 at 6:45 p.m. at my home. It was a lovely backyard wedding. I wish them well. Zachary is home. He needs help obtaining work. I referred him to the City of SB Department.

9/2/93

The Rehab Fair went very good. I met a lot of people, exchanged business cards. I hope to receive a lot of referrals. I need to move downstairs. I placed a call to Jeff awaiting his return call. Curtis and I checked out the suites downstairs. I would like unit B & C, he likes A. Hopefully we can get a good deal since they have been vacant for over a year.

I must write Wilbert. I referred Zachary to the City of SB for training. I pray He follows through. Lord, thank You for the connections I have made. I pray that FDSA continues to grow and prosper.

Thank You, Jesus. Linda

9/6/93

Visited Loveland Church and The Church of The Living God yesterday. Pastor Dowdy told me he had signed my contract with the City for training as a vendor. Lord, thank You!

9/7/93 ~ 5:07 p.m.

Received a call from Victorville — another student that makes 3. Thank You, Jesus. Tomorrow Adenia and I make a presentation to the Colton office. I pray for positive responses and support from the staff. I must move. Lord, guide me to my new location. End this lease so that I may make an expedient smooth transition. I pray for the bundle of rehab clients. Lord, guide me on this path. I pray that my meeting with San Bernardino Community Hospital is positive with supplies, and contract for training students in the Route Aide Program.

Lord, thank You.

Linda L. Smith

9/15/93 ~ 2:50 p.m.

Had lunch today with Mr. Keith Lee. The Lord is blessing us. I will possibly receive the Riverside contract. San Bernardino is coming and the County will send more this year. I pray for focus, improved knowledge, and management.

I think of Michelle often. I miss her dearly.

Today I leave for the God's Women's Conference (GWC). This will be a blessed trip. Thank You, Lord. Guide us and protect us from all harm. Embrace us with Your love and protection.

9/20/93 ~ 8:15 a.m.

Lord, thank You for this wonderful weekend. The God's Women's Conference was blessed and was a blessing for me.

I received the approval from Riverside County JTPA! I will be moving downstairs within a month and a half...

Lord, guide me.

9/20/93 ~ 5:55 p.m.

Well Lord, I thank You for the Riverside County Contract. The hospital I needed and wanted declined my proposal for training. I will seek a new location. I pray that I am in tune. I need to grow in marketing, developing a package.

Pam's father is ill. I pray for a healing and blessing for him. I pray that the Lord comfort her and her family.

10/2/93 ~ 11:25 a.m.

I thank God for this day! I thank Him for my peace, joy, happiness, my appreciation of life, and my kindness towards others. I thank Him for loving me, guiding me, and carrying me.

I received notice of acceptance with Riverside County for $144,000. I pray that we are effective and efficient in our process. Lord, guide us through the years ahead.

I interviewed a young lady for RN instructor. If the Lord is willing, she will become part of our family here.

Lord, I ask for the knowledge, wisdom, leadership, and the work ethic I need to do Your work. I pray for a blessing for a new location. Lord, I don't know how to fairly and peacefully (within) move from here, but I know I must move. I must go forward. Guide me to a new location. I believe I will receive a new location with rent less than $1,200 and plenty of space for staff and classes. I claim a new location that is built for my needs. Thank You, Jesus, for the new location You have bestowed upon me. I claim it in the name of Jesus.

Now as I write this paper for Riverside County on our organization for the new session, Lord, guide me. Control the thoughts I think and the words I write.

Thank You, Jesus. Your Child, Linda

10/4/93 ~ 8:25 p.m.

Lord, I thank You. Last night I prayed with Julie. Lord, thank You for guiding me, for my contracts. Today, I made an appointment with Jim at SB Hospital to receive equipment! I pray for a new office. Thank You.

I claim a new site, affordable, in the name of Jesus.

Julie, thank you for your love, prayers and support. Thank You, Jesus.

10/11/13 ~ 2:25 p.m.

Last week was a busy and blessed week. I met Ted Holt on Wednesday, October 6th. I contacted him after Riverside JTPA Director said he would not accept the San Bernardino site as a training site for Riverside clients. Mr. Holt, hearing the urgency in my voice, scheduled an appointment. Thanks to Ted, I hopefully will have a space in the city of Riverside, two blocks from the Hospital. I will pick up the agreement on Wednesday and turn it in to the JTPA office. I pray to start a class by November 15th.

I went to SB Community Hospital to pick out items for school sites. I felt like a kid in a toy store. What a list: chairs, desks, beds, typewriter, microwave, fridge, chalkboard, and linen.

Lord, enable me to always do what is RIGHT. I pray to maintain a clean heart, mind, and a good spirit. Thank You for the guidance. Enable me to generate the revenue FDSA needs to be successful financially. I pray for wisdom, knowledge, contact of Christian instructors, and a well received, organized school and programs.

All I can say is Thank You, Jesus. All I can do is call Your name, Jesus, Jesus, Jesus.

I called to talk with Ernell. He is a good listener. I am blessed to have a friend like him.

10/13/93 ~ 8:55 a.m.

MY LORD, last night I talked with my daddy. My father, Walter Russ, was a spiritual man. I love talking with him on expressing how good God is. How important it is to stand firm in faith. My father prayed for me — Oh, Halleluiah! I know I am doing God's work.

Yesterday I received 3 loads of items from San Bernardino Community Hospital: chairs, desks, lamps, fridge, wheel chairs, end tables, over bed tables. Oh, what a blessing. I will receive the hospital agreement, the rental agreement, and the Riverside County Contract!

The Lord is God. He is Good.

10/16/93 ~ 11:25 a.m.

On this day, I give praises to God. Thanks for my students, the school, contracts, family, friends, quality of my life. Heavenly Father, I pray for a RN to teach the Riverside class. I pray she is knowledgeable of Christ, flexible, kind, considerate. I pray for beds and a new location.

Thank You for this day. Amen. Back to class.

10/22/93 ~ 5:45 p.m.

On Tuesday, the Lord sent blessings. I interviewed an RN interested in doing the in-service program. I received a call from the JTPA office—a check is coming.

Received a call from an RN in Riverside. She is scheduled for an interview on Monday, October 25th. San Bernardino Community Hospital provided me with pillows, sheets, and pillow cases and asked if I needed anything else... God is good!

Linda L. Smith

The Council is coming November 9th. Just in time. Lord, I pray that all is well. I claim Victory in the Name of Jesus.

We have 8-10 persons scheduled for class on Monday! We are advertising in Riverside with good responses.

Thank You, God, for a blessed week.

10/26/93

Yesterday, I received four calls for referrals: Victorville, 1; SB County, 2 (I had to reject one), and Ontario, 1.

I received my extension from the Credential board till October 1994! Thank God.

Today, the Ontario referral came in and she will enroll into November 15th class. That is 5 now with 3 weeks to go!

Today Suzanne White from Riverside JTPA called and things look fine. Contract to be signed Thursday or Friday. She will be reassigned November 8th. God kept her in place to help me! What a blessing she was and is.

I pray for Success, the ability to manage my company, meet financial needs, grow, teach others and help improve their lives!

God, thanks for a firm hand on me. I trust in the Lord for all of my needs. I ask and receive.

10/28/93 ~ 2:35 p.m.

Lord have mercy, I jump with joy!

Friday, I met with Shirley about rental in Riverside. We'll be able to move in this weekend. I signed the clinical agreement with Ted Holt at CCH. They are due for survey and I claim victory in Jesus name for a positive hospital survey. They will not receive any citations.

I met with Suzanna, such a nice Lady! She truly has been a blessing working with FDSA, getting our contract together. I pray that I sign it tomorrow.

The Lord has blessed me with two nurses for hire. One for Riverside, the other for San Bernardino/Placement. I pray for revenue to support staff and all business operations.

Today San Bernardino City called and said my contract is ready for pick up. God, guide me and keep me focused. You supply all of my needs. I pray for staff, growth, and support among each other. I am filled with joy.

11/1/93 ~ 6:30 p.m.

The Lord is Good. Stay fast in faith and He will provide and guide.

Today I signed the City of San Bernardino contract. Nancy said I could use her building for training. I signed the lease on Riverside. The Riverside contract is coming! Thank You, Jesus!

Robert Rochelle is back. He called and has two clients.

Lord, keep me focused in spiritual form always. Enable me to be a sound, mindful spiritual leader. Guide me to the right path. I pray that we as a team are able to provide the best training for our clients that we can and will make a difference in their lives. That we are always respectful and supportive of one another. In Jesus name, I pray for those things and I claim victory in His name.

11/9/93

I sat here awaiting the visit from the council. I am ready. Yesterday, I received the Riverside contract, I signed four. and will return them back tomorrow.

Yesterday, Walter and Zack helped me move items from the SB storage to Riverside site. Lord, what a blessed day.

I met with the instructors on Thursday, the 4th. I marvel at our growth this past year. God has truly guided me on a magnificent trip. I stand on faith, for I know I have done nothing alone. The pieces of the puzzle continue to fit into place. I have such peace in knowing that all will be good — all right.

11/10/93 ~ 5:00 p.m.

Mr. Davis (council) did not show up yesterday. I stayed until 5:30 p.m. Too tired to drive to SB for a meeting. I went home.

I spoke with Mr. Davis today; there was a mix up with the schedule. He has the school papers on the Riverside site, which will be listed as a satellite. I received, signed, and returned my contract to Riverside.

12-13 persons showed up for the first orientation. Things went smoothly. The room needed a little work: more lights, drapes needed cleaning, but we are ready.

I thank God for this opportunity to give aide to others. I am grateful for my staff and the continued blessings to come.

PEACE. BE STILL.

11/12/93 ~ 3:15 p.m.

I had fun today with the students. It is a joy to see them respond as the concepts of theory are being learned. I am happy.

Shirley has been a blessing and a big help. She will do very well in the program as an instructor.

Things work out for the best — always!

11/23/93 ~ 7:50 a.m.

Last Tuesday, November 16th, I received, signed, and delivered the Riverside contract. I am so grateful to God for this blessing. The orientations have been going well. We should have 15 students for the 29th class. I thank God for all of His blessings. I hired a new clerk yesterday. I pray she is of good heart and work well with us.

God is good and His mercy is everlasting.

Guide us this day.

11/28/93 ~ 1:50 p.m.

I sit today watching the clouds move across the sky and thinking how magnificent God is! To behold His beauty, His works, to know that I am a tool He designed. I have a purpose, a goal, and a mission.

And through Him, all things are possible. I trust Him. I have unquestionable faith in His power to do all and provide all.

I have less than $900 in my checking account and $1,700 in my savings. My bills exceed $5,000. I can't worry about where the money is coming from, for God is my Source, my Provider. I thank Him for my staff. He has given me what I need and He will continue to provide opportunities for FDSA, and me, as I have grown to maturity in my position. I know I am safe with my Lord, Jesus.

Oh Heavenly Father, I thank You. Guide me along the way. I pray to always seek to help others, that greed never enters into my mind nor overcome my objectives. I pray for each staff member, for their financial growth, for their love of You, for peace and harmony in their homes.

Thank You, Jesus, for this opportunity to help others. It is a privilege and honor for I know You could have chosen another.

12/1/93 ~ 5:55 p.m.

☺ Riverside accepted our first set of invoices. I don't know what to write. I am so happy. Thank You, Jesus! I will be able to pay bills, salaries, provide assistance at my home! I am so grateful to God.

The classes are going well...

12/8/93 ~ 5:30 p.m.

I received a call from the first Norton Air Force Base referral! The San Bernardino, and the Riverside programs are going well.

I thank God for this day, for He has brought me through yesterday!

I know that I know that He guides, protects, and provides for FDSA and me. Last week, my checkbook was down to less than $200.80. Payroll, rent, and bills are due. I continue to stand on faith that God will provide. Payroll will be met, rents are paid, bills we be covered. Donna has given me the tickets for our Jamaica flight. Ernell and I are going in April (1st-7th). I am very grateful for her generosity and kindness.

Thank You, Jesus, for Everything!

12/16/93 ~ 5:00 p.m.

I give praise to my Lord Jesus. Today has been a blessed day. Every day is a blessed day. I signed up four students for the next class. I met with Ms. Keller at SB Com. Hospital... Praise the Lord! I will be able to use the Hospital as a clinical training site for the Acute Nurse Aide Program. God has been good to Four-D Success Academy. I pray to obtain at least four computers soon. I am seeking donations. I know the Lord will have me to move. I wait to be pointed in the right direction.

We are busy. Last year at this time, I had five students total. Today I have 29 enrolled and preparing for a class of 15 in two weeks. Home Health is going to pick up! Thank You, Lord.

12/20/93 ~ 11:50 p.m.

On Saturday, a check for $10,000 came in from S.B. County. Thank You, Jesus!

Imagine I have a staff of two secretaries, one accountant, two full-time, and two part-time instructors, and one volunteer instructor.

I am seeking computers and in prayer for a new location after I have received the approval from Mr. Davis and Department of Health Services (DHS). He called to say Riverside was okay. My letter should arrive this week.

Christmas is this Saturday, Praise the Lord for His love, grace, and guidance.

12/21/93 ~ 12:35 p.m.

I picked up the County (SB) check for $3,680. I paid all of my bills and made payroll. One must take time to STOP and PRAISE THE LORD!

I signed up to Adopt-A-Family through church. I have called twice and left messages with my phone number. I hope they call back. I wish to purchase food for the family.

I am tired. God, strengthen me, refresh me.

San Bernardino Community Hospital turned down my agreement for Acute Aide Training. I applied for a position as house supervisor. With God's blessing, the VP of Clinical Services will change his mind.

12/23/93 ~ 5:19 p.m.

Lord, I thank You for this day! I Thank You, Jesus for allowing me to do this work. I am grateful for my staff and students.

Today, I interviewed with Mr. Sims for a supervisory position at San Bernardino Community Hospital. I will begin to work there in January. Also, the Acute CNA class will take place. He's leaning to the left in favor of FDSA. God is good. Knowing what His plan is for me and following it brings me great joy. I know what I do is directly related to Him! He guides me, and I stand by faith. Through grace, I will continue to grow, and this school will make a way for others. I bathe in His glory.

Praises to God on High...

Happy Holidays to all!

Linda Smith

12/24/93 ~ 3:45 p.m.

Received a check for $33,000 from Riverside. Today, my husband will be given back funds he has provided to aide in keeping Four-D Success Academy open. God, I thank You. Thank You for blessing

the school, me, my staff, family members and friends. Thank You,
Linda

1/3/94

I am here. God, thank You. A New Year, new goals, and new
inspirations. I am thankful for 1993, I paid more than bills, and I
created an avenue for others to improve their lives. I lived by example.
I am overwhelmed with joy. I am here!

Faith brought me through. I sit here and reflect on where I was in
September 1992. Only Pam and I, and we did the work of five people.
Taught class, marketing, phones, files, and ran, ran, ran! These
were times I know the Lord carried me. I needed strength; I needed to
stay in the light. Bills mounted up and I simply gave them to the
Lord. Today FDSA has three clinical sites operating. San
Bernardino, Riverside, and Claremont. There are three full-time
instructors, two secretaries, one accountant, two part-time
instructors and me. Last year we enrolled 32 students through SB
County JTPA. Today we have enrolled 47 with the potential
enrollment of 45 more. 1994 will triple 1993 from 32 to 96.

The Home Health program will triple this year.

The Acute Nurse Aide Program has been accepted by San
Bernardino Community Hospital. I know this program will be a
success in enrollees seeking employment opportunities in Acute
Training.

Lord, I thank You for a blessed year. I thank You for speaking to me,
guiding me, I pray to continue to do this work, and if it is Your will I
will open a Licensed Vocational Nurse (LVN) program.

I am filled with joy. I am making a difference in someone's life.

1/8/94 ~ 3:20 p.m.

Earlier this week, we had our first monitoring visit by Riverside. We were ready! Systems in place, answers given. Account books in order. We were told we are ahead of the game. We had one of the best systems and thorough processes seen. We were given advice on several things. But overall, we looked good! With the positive report from the monitoring, FDSA would end up with a larger contract next year. Wednesday, I met with the administrator at Palamares. They need to have training for their Respiratory Technician Aide soon. A possible contract coming up.

Monday the 10th, we began orientation for the second group of students.

Friday, with peace, calmness, I pay bills, staff, MYSELF, and have money in the account. God, thank You.

1/21/94 ~ 10:00 a.m.

A class graduated yesterday. How strange it is that some people are not grateful for all that You do. One student did not say thank you to the instructor, and she didn't even say goodbye! But for all the others, to see the smiles of accomplishment, I would go through it all over again. We had a nice luncheon at the Radisson in SB.

SB County indicated the possibility of additional funds for training. If this happens I hope to enroll 15 - 30 students.

God, strengthen me. I feel tired, sometimes weary. I received a $4,000+ insurance bill. This just overwhelmed me. This has not been a good morning.

Lord, guide me and keep me focused. Give me the knowledge and tools I need to be successful. Your Child, Linda

1/26/94

This has been a very stressful day. Cynthia Garey in Sacramento refuses to accept my clinical skills checklist although it has been reviewed and approved by four other people from licensing.

God, strengthen me and guide me. I pray that she doesn't interfere with the Riverside program. I truly turn toward to God. I ask that He shield FDSA against the enemy for I know Satan is very hungry. He wants to destroy hopes, dreams, and lives. I know that God is almighty. He is capable of raising me above all turmoil and strife.

Tomorrow will be a better joy-filled blessed day.

I pray that Ms. Luna see clearly the ways of Mr. Gary and hold her action for not only FDSA's sake, but for all who must report to her. Amen!

1/31/94 ~ 6:50 p.m.

God brought Rev. Jeff Morehead into my life. I was referred to him by Keith Lee. I was seeking a new space to relocate. Mr. Morehead has a building located at the Norton Air force base. With God's blessing, we will relocate there.

Cynthia Garey rejected the skills checklist for the second time. May Ann and I redid it. Hopefully it will be okay.

I prayed to God that He removes all adversaries, that I am attentive and focused on the vision of FDSA. I pray for protection, I pray that the Riverside site is approved without a visit. Oh God, grant me this blessing.

2/3/94

Yesterday I felt full, sad, and overwhelmed. Thoughts of Michelle Daisy ran through my mind and brought such a depth of sadness I cried as if she had passed yesterday.

I resubmitted the skills checklist. I will await Cynthia Garey's response. Mr. Davis (council) called. He will be here on the 9th. God, be with me.

I met with Rev. Jeff Morehead. He and I will work together, I will move to Norton in May. God, Guide FDSA.

Today, the Riverside Class Graduated with a group. I received a lovely hand-painted picture of an Angel from Teresa for it represented me to them! Shirley received a plaque with all their names. Flowers were also given. We had a wonderful time at the Radisson Hotel.

Thank You, Jesus!

2/9/94

Thank You, Lord! Today Mr. David Davis reviewed files and documented the site. He gave verbal approval, which will be good through 2/97. Lord, Mr. Davis gave referral info to me for Compton site training. He will inquire about relocation the most economical way!

I am still unable to reach Cynthia Garey. I need her approval for Riverside. I pray to God for guidance. I ask that He touches her heart, that she finds favor in Four-D Success Academy.

I am filled with Joy. Julie Ballard called today. She's making arrangements for a female group retreat. We need to sit still and pray! I look forward to it.

2/12/94 ~ 1:50 p.m.

Today, I met Jean Eiber. She was referred by Nancy Sedlack. Lord, thank You. Jean and I will be working together to develop a LVN program.

This I submit in prayer:

I pray for a way to financially establish scholarships for students. Some may be able to pay for their education, but for those who can't, Lord show me how to provide for them.

I pray that the approving board accepts our application the first time around.

I pray that the Norton site comes through so we can move in by June.

I pray that San Bernardino Community Hospital allows us to use it as a training site.

I pray for the staff needed to do all those things You envision me to do.

I pray for staff of good heart, Christian understanding, and love.

I claim victory in the name of Jesus. I walk by faith, for I know He is underneath me, above me, and around me. I am protected from all adversaries. For what I do, I do as God instructs.

Heavenly Father. Thank You for giving me the opportunity to help others.

2/21/94

On Tuesday 2/15/94, Cynthia Garey put me through a full survey for Riverside. She put the program on hold. Lord, I've gone through the storm (Mark 4:35-41) and I came out on the other side. Thank

Linda L. Smith

You for Your guidance, and for strengthening me. Thank You for the messages I've received. Keep me focused, renew my strength, give me wisdom and knowledge to continue to do Your work.

I am saddened to have the program on hold, yet I get filled with joy in knowing Jesus is carrying me through all the turmoil.

I'm being groomed for something bigger.

2/27/94

I sit here thinking about the future. I think of goals to aim for, establishing a strong LVN Program, improving present programs… CNA, HHA, Inservices, and establishing a scholarship for the LVN Program called simply "We Care Scholarship". On a plaque we will engrave the names of those that have helped FDSA achieve its goals by helping others:

Ernell Smith

Advisory Council Members

Beverly Wilson

Keith Lee

Virgil Norby

Staff of FDSA

Elizabeth Duncan

Robert Rochelle

SBC

Riverside JTPA

To the many who gave words of support and prayers, one day this will be! Although Riverside is still on hold, I forge ahead to new avenues.

I have spoken with the City of Compton JTPA possible school site in June.

The Continued Education program is going well. Improvements needed, challenges to be met, but the future is bright.

I have a spirit of peace, for I know God watches over me and in His presence all is always well.

Patience is a virtue; He has bigger things in store for FDSA and me. I pray to be focused, attentive and prepared.

Thank You, Jesus, for this day.

3/7/94 ~ 5:35

We received approval from DHS for Riverside on Friday. I was packed and ready to fly out on Thursday. I spoke with Ms. Luna who made it quite clear she would not see me and I had to wait for Cynthia Garey's report. Andrea called Riverside to report I was operating fraudulently.

I received a call from Loren, I explained the problem with her and all is well. She even wanted me to give her the toll free number to CNA Board.

Andrea has not returned the COPES Test she took from the office on the Riverside students. She must return the school's property before receiving her final check

I am going through an audit, and I am not pleased with Curtis at this time. Riverside billing due two months ago for February and

March. The county budget is due today and not done. Items discussed. I will not tolerate poor performance.

Computers came in today. I shall assess over the next month for improvements. Dawn Grimes is now the full-time receptionist.

Lord, thank You for this day. I need guidance, strength, and wisdom.

Help me to be the best manager I can be. Thank You.

3/9/94 ~ 4:55

I purchased two computers yesterday, a step into the 21st century! And I can't wait to complete all the financial audits for, SB City, SB County, and Riverside.

I was approved for $35,000 SBA, and I received a master card charge plate. Life is busy and God continues to guide me.

3/12/94

What a week! The Riverside site is approved! The computers came in. Andrea brought her brother on the 10th and he did all the talking. I informed him that my business had nothing to do with him. She refuses to return the COPES. I have filled out the necessary paperwork to take her to small claims court.

Today Jean, Cherry and I met to discuss the LVN Program. We are on our way. God is good! Jean will accept payment after the first student enrolls. I am excited. I pray for a new location.

3/21/94

I went to the mountain to pray, and reunite with the Lord and rest. I thank Julie so much for her time and attention. God spoke to me and all is alright. I was given a location to move to. It is in San

Bernardino on E Street at 15 cents a square foot. I seek 5,000 square feet and God is my guide! Today, on my desk is the contract from the SB County for $60,000. Thank You, Jesus, I know I will be extremely busy over the next three months. But I have the strength and the desire to carry on.

Lord, thank You.

3/25/94 ~ 4:40 p.m.

After reviewing the information about the financial recordings, I find myself in a state of disbelief. How could this be? Yet it is good that the audit is bringing these problems out now. There are no reasons given for substandard performance by Curtis. My concerns are the numerous errors with deposits, recordings, lack of follow through, late reports for taxes, and tardiness. I assess negligence. Time is available — working full-time. Today, he was informed that the Smith's taxes would be done by Myra Greg (CPA). I could not afford to have FDSA affect my home and Ernell's business. Curtis informed me he had a written resignation. I informed him that if presented, I would accept it. He needs more time to work on his business. It was agreed that April 8th or 11th would be his last day. Starting Monday, April 28th he will work part-time, preferably 8-12. He never arrives by 8 a.m. He will be paid for hours worked.

I know God helped me though this management process. I had such PEACE in my heart, mind, thoughts, and the words I spoke. I know I will find or have delivered a Christian, honest, knowledgeable, good accountant.

Ammenah Fuller Medical Records called to say she is still interested in coming on board. We meet April 18th at 10:00 a.m.

81

March 28th, we have another class starting. It is funded through additional money from SB Co. We have tripled in size. I have gone from a staff of two to seven. We have three approved training sites: Claremont, San Bernardino and Riverside. We have trained or enrolled 110 CNA/HHA students thus far, and have two more classes scheduled.

I have Peace today.

4/11/94

Well, since the last entry, I have been to Jamaica! What a wonderful week alone with my husband! Donna provided for the Airfare, we paid for the hotel. A dream vacation come true! There is much to do back at work, but the staff maintained things.

Saturday the 9th, Ernell drove me to see Sadiq. It was a very pleasant trip. He looks good. God is watching over him.

I hired a new (full-time) instructor, Brenda Perry LVN. There were nine students for the first class at the Hilton. Lord, double the number for the 23rd class.

God, thank You!

4/16/94

A week back and I feel like I need another vacation. Curtis resigned at my request. His performance lacked the levels to meet FDSA standards. We are preparing for 30 students to start on the 25th. Time is going by so fast! Students are coming and going. There are 17 students enrolled into the HHA Class1, the first class at the Hilton went well.

I pray the contracts are renewed for the upcoming year. We all have worked hard to be successful. I pray to become a better manager of this business.

4/21/94

Today, Cherry and I visited SBCH, met with Teresa Mitchell for the Acute Nurse Aide Program. Things are set to start May 9th. Left clinical affiliation with Mr. Sims, secretary for the LVN program.

Received a possible site for Riverside. With a little work, it will be a good training site.

God, just put things in place. All I need to do is wait, be patient, and follow. So many good things can come of this work. So many people to help. Lord, grant us the wisdom and knowledge we need to do this work which You have guided me into.

I pray that Four-D Success Academy will become a highly recognized training institute. A school with integrity, and performance. I pray that our graduates are outstanding in their work and easily recognizable through their performance and productivity.

Lord, I pray for a highly skilled, qualified bookkeeper. I pray for a licensed, devoted staff to instruct our courses.

Thank You, Jesus for Your love, patience, and guidance.

I pray for wisdom, knowledge, and success.

5/5/94 ~ 4:55 p.m.

We all are working so hard, I feel physically ill. My feet are swollen and painful today. The doctor put me on meds and ran a lot of tests.

I have been teaching the Riverside class and Shirley is preparing for the next group. Cherry is preparing for the Acute Class, Mary is preparing for the insurance class. Adenia and Betty are busy teaching the SB CNA/HHA classes, and Pam and Dawn are running the office.

I thank God for my team. I give thanks to our united goal to help others. Our commitment to Four-D Success. Ladies, I thank you. I had prayed to have $60,000 in the account and I have it. I am looking at a new training site in Riverside. Looking for a new site in SB and possibly Upland or Rancho Cucamonga. I have much to learn and God will guide me. It's a joy to do this work.

Now, Happy Mother's day to all. I am going to Lake Mead to relax, relax, relax, and fish.

5/13/94

Today is a blessed day! On Tuesday, I received the Acute Hospital Affiliation with San Bernardino Com. Hospital. Jesus, people said I would not get it, but they do not know my God and what He has set for Four-D Success Academy.

There are good things planned for the future LVN Programs and Medical Records Program. Increased participation for Inservice, HHA and Acute Aide Program. Increased enrollment for the CNA class, and staff benefits. God, thank You.

Deposits made this year to date = $ 179,404.47 I am shocked! I sit and know God is really REAL — this is His work for I am only His support.

We had a good staff meeting today. We started with a prayer. We must end with prayer.

Heavenly Father, I pray for guidance. Keep us on track within the light. Soften our hearts toward the uncaring, promote good cheer and spirit from us all. Enable us to always work in peace. Keep this team together mentally and spiritually.

Better ME... Groom ME. I feel Your presence in my life. Thank You for this opportunity to help others. Thank You for my family, love, and support.

God, thank You. Your Child in Christ Jesus, Linda

5/23/94 ~ 2:15 p.m.

Thank You, Jesus for a blessed year! So much has happened; the Acute Training program is going well with four students. The Continued Education classes average seven students. My goal and prayer is for 20. The Home Health class will start up in June.

Cherry has been working on the LVN Program with Jean Eiber. Adenia and Shirley are assisting with placement. Pam and Dawn are a good team in the office. We are establishing new operations for the upcoming year.

I seldom think about how much we have received in dollars until I have to do an audit or proposal. I do look at the financials but I never have actually seen the figure. Possibly, because I am not interested in financial gain for myself, or because I know Jesus will provide all my needs and those of Four-D Success Academy. This past weekend, I spent in fellowship for Pastor Dowdy's 3rd Anniversary. It was a blessing to hear about manifesting one's vision that the Lord has given.

I know my vision comes from the Lord. He gives us what we can handle. I pray for continued growth. I am reporting $298,000 in current fiscal year earning from SB City and SB County. We will have received $144,000 from Riverside County by 8/30/94, and approximately $7,000 from other sources. $449,000 this year! Jesus, Jesus, Jesus, thank You. I claim 1994-1995 as a blessed year. A year to reach out and help others. A year to provide the LVN class at no cost to others. I claim a training site in SB.

Thank You, Lord.

5/26/94 ~ 6:15 p.m.

The Lord is good, all the time!

I am awaiting the outcome of the Riverside proposal. I claim Victory in the name of Jesus. Today I looked again at the new Jurupa site. It should be remodeled by June 30th. I am seeking a new location in San Bernardino. God will open up the door for the new training site.

The first portion of the LVN Program went to Marcia (consultant) before I reviewed it. We will not send information out that is not clear in print and does not represent FDSA. A lot of calls are coming in for the LVN Program. The work in the Continued Education Class delights me. I am proud of US! I sit here feeling at peace. I have prayed in the quiet of my office. I pray daily but there are times I must sit, be still, and realize how great He is, how far I have come, and look to where I am going and say, "Thank You for choosing me to do this wonderfully rewarding task." Today, I paid over $5,000 in payroll. Lord, I know through You, all things are possible. I know so little about accounting, but I know You are my banker!

Guide me and give me the knowledge I need to do Your work.

Your Child in Christ Jesus

5/29/94 ~ 1:35 p.m.

On Friday the 27th, I picked up an agreement from the bank for a $35,000 line of credit! I've deposited $40,000 this month, bills are paid, and God is good!

I am in prayer for a new site in SB. I must move from the Public Enterprise Center. I pray to remain until the end of July. By then, God will have a new place for me.

Lord, keep me focused on the vision, keep me attentive to Your messages. Give me the knowledge I need to succeed.

Donna asked me what books I read to get this business started. All I could do was smile for I've not read any books — You are the Author of my mind. Thank You for this day.

6/3/94 ~ 6:30 p.m.

I am seeking a new location in San Bernardino. I don't even question how I will pay the rent. God takes care of ALL things. As I drove around SB looking for a space, writing addresses and phone numbers, I realized I was looking at a large building, 6,000 sq. ft. Lord, what is our future? I began to pray for guidance, giving thanks for what He has done for the school, the calmness I felt inside, and for knowing He is my Banker. His funds are endless and I have no financial worries in this world. People will ask me how much do I want to pay for rent. I smile and say I haven't thought of it, I only know what I need. My Source will care for it.

Lord, I pray that our seats are filled, our space is adequate, our aim is high, our spirit is right, our focus is not selfish, our love is genuine, and our faith is solely in You!

Linda L. Smith

Today I received the package to incorporate from Greg. There is much work to do. Peace be unto You and let it multiply. Mary Salim brought in a scripture for me, Ephesians 3:20... it says God is able to provide ABUNDANTLY above all that we ask or think according to the POWER that works in US!

Four-D Success received the Board of Registered Nurses (BRN) Provider number! This allows FDSA to provide Continued education classes. God, thank You!

6/7/94 ~ 10:15

Yesterday the security guard locked Sherry out of the class. Some misunderstanding as to why/how we got into the classroom.

Glenda and Alea have truly been a blessing to FDSA and me. They worked and open the doors for us. The class will be held tonight.

Jean and Cherry are having what I call an intellectual debate on the structure of the LVN Program. How interesting. I am the buffer and final decision maker. 100% of Betty's students passed the state test on 6/4/94! God is truly blessing FDSA! Faith, patience, belief in His holy words. Nothing is impossible, all things are possible — ask and receive. Jesus, thank You for Your magnificent wonders.

Love Your Child, Linda

6/9/94 ~ 5:35 p.m.

God's plan is so wonderful. Mike called with a possible building. I will go see it next week. Scheduled an appointment with an experienced nurse interested in teaching one of our part-time evening classes. Jesus, this is great!

Lord, thank You, I pray never to doubt You, I will follow You. Continue to guide me and aid FDSA in its growth.

I thank You for my joy, my staff, my LIFE!

Remove ALL obstacles.

Philippians 4:13- I can do all things through Christ which strengthen me!!

All things ...

Yes, Lord!

6/15/94 & 6/16/94 ~ 1:50 p.m.

Today is a blessed day, like every day. FDSA received a $35,000 line of credit with the bank. I received a wonderful blessing yesterday. The Riverside student stood for prayer before starting class. This was truly an affirmation from God that what we do here at FDSA is for the right reasons. God will guide us and provide for us.

I received referrals to Kaiser DSD for the LVN Program via (Skip, SB JTPA member). I found a copier for $600. This is $3,700 less thun the new one I was looking at.

God is good.

Jane Singleton and I discussed a Youth Program for FDSA.

God will unite us and guide us in Jesus Name, Amen.

Today, my baby is 16,

Happy Birthday Aisha Linell Smith!

6/18/94 ~ 3:00 p.m.

Yesterday, Four-D Success Academy provided group Medical Insurance Coverage for its staff of 6 full-time employees. Jesus is so good! Words can't express my happiness and joy. I just pray that He continues to provide our needs, that our LVN Program is approved the first time around in His name. I pray that our instructors are of God's spirit and of good will. He will provide all our needs.

Today we have an Acute class, HHA class, and a Continued Ed Class going. Thank You, Jesus.

Today, Ernell bought us our new copier for $600. The old one will go to Riverside.

7/1/94 ~ 1:40 p.m.

Since my last entry, much has happened. Yesterday, I signed the S.B. City Contract for 1994-1995. There were actually six contracts with a couple lasting until June 1996!

I found a location in downtown S.B. on 5th St. Lord, I knew it was there. Thank You for guiding me. I know I can't worry about the cost of rent for You are my Provider and rent payer!! Riverside is coming along. I will inspect it on Tuesday the 5th. Today, I sum up the checking account balance of $90,085.04. Lord, thank You. This is four months operating cost!

Yesterday, Riverside and SB classes graduated 22 students! What a joy to see the smiling faces and the guests. There were about 70 people in all. We are busy getting ready for the future. Lord, I see my advisory team dwindling. Please send me spiritual and knowledgeable replacements.

Thank You for 1993-1994.

Michelle, I miss you.

7/1/94 ~ 2:55 p.m.

$108,655.84 in the checking account.

Thank You, Lord!

7/7/94 ~ 3:38 p.m.

Yesterday, FDSA received its corporate papers. We have received facility agreements from Hill Haven in SB for the CNA and LVN program. The Riverside site looks good. Today I had lunch with Mr. K. Lee. I explained the LVN Program and the desire to open a daycare within the school. He was interested and recommended I pursue the programs.

I am excited about the future.

Jesus, I thank You!

7/8/94

Today, I filed the paperwork to submit factious names: Four-D Success Academy, Inc.

How nice.

I have inquired about a child care center for the school in the SB Site. How wonderful it would be to service student and child on the same premises.

Ernell is on a camping trip with "men and boys."

The girls are out this afternoon and I am leaving to visit Donna. This has been a blessed week. Thank You, Jesus, for Your love for me, for the blessings and the gift to share.

Your child, Linda

7/13/94 ~ 4:30 p.m.

The Almighty God is good. Today, we received the notification for approval of $272,000 for the Riverside Contract. The Riverside site will be completed by 7/15/94 for us to move in.

I sit here and cry, giving thanks and praises to the Lord. He has given (provided) me an opportunity to train for "free".

Keep me focused. Let me walk always in Your light.

Yesterday, my father had an angioplasty. Whatever the results, he and I know God is able. Dad feels good and if the Lord calls him home we are okay for we know heaven awaits him.

7/21/94 ~ 7:40 p.m.

I've been busy. Today, I turned in the Riverside contract (revised for budget) and the SB Co. contracts. Lord, I thank You for these blessings. We have class starting 7/26/94 and may have 10+ students. Riverside starts 8/1/94 with 17 students.

I am praying and looking for a new site in the SB area. I've looked in Cooley Ranch area. Lord guide and aide me in finding a place. The PEPC is not allowing my evening class to continue. Actually, it's the EDA office. Time is short but just know the Lord will provide.

Focus, peace, internal calmness, knowledge, joy, and love.

I have much to do. Lord, help me pull it together!

7/23/94 ~ 3:40 p.m.

Today, Ernell, Aisha, and Walter moved Four-D Success Academy, Inc. into its new site in Riverside. We obtained a 2073 sq. ft. space.

God is good.

The students will truly be able to move around in a more spacious and relaxing environment.

I am thankful for the 400 square feet space we had for a year.

I must transfer the phone lines and put up pictures and plants.

The Corporation's paper came with the fictitious notice. It is strange to see Linda L. Smith President. Who would have known — no one but Jesus!

I am tired, and I write as so — Go rest, pray, and rejuvenate.

7/24/94 ~ 8:10 p.m.

Praise the Lord Almighty. Today, I organized the Riverside site. What a joy to see where God has taken the school. We have gone from a 400 sq. ft. space to 2,073 sq. ft.

Aisha has been hired by McDonald's, and Tahira waits to hear from Mervyn's. Lord, bless her with a job.

This week is going to be busy. I must find a new site for the Acute Class and for the SB Training Classes. God, guide me and bless the school.

Love Your Child, Linda

7/25/94

Tahira was hired by Mervyn's today. Tomorrow she will start the CNA Class.

7/29/94 ~ 5:10 p.m.

This is the end of the journal and the beginning of another.

July 29th, San Bernardino started with eight students, on August 11th. Riverside will start with 18 students.

Linda L. Smith

I am working with Charlie Seymour on doing a commercial. Mike is still looking into Colton for a new training site. I visited a new daycare site this week, and obtained books and new ideals for set up. This is going to be a project. Jesus, thanks a lot!

Today, I received the San Bernardino Co. contract and earlier this week I received the City of San Bernardino Contract.

My current bank statement ending July 18, 1994 showing a daily balances of $100,000 for 3 days plus. Yeah, God!

Looking Back …

- It has been said that knowledge is power. From a child, all I ever wanted to do was make a difference in the life of another. *I am going to become a nurse,* I told myself at a young age. My steps have been decisive, as I not only fulfilled my childhood dream, but I have successfully expanded my dream into becoming an educator that empowers others through knowledge as it pertains to the field of medicine.

- The journey has not always been smooth, as I have sought to empower others through knowledge. The institution of my family has been threatened, and time would not only test the strength of our foundation, but it challenged our faith and belief in the vision that I believe God Himself gave to my whole family and me.

- Snippets of success are certain to come, and I had to remember to celebrate in that moment, cry tears of joy, and immediately get back to working the plan. And it was a big plan that kept my faith engaged and totally dependent on the Lord to guide my way!

- I have learned throughout the years to trust the vision no matter what it looks like! I didn't realize the magnitude of my potential and actions at the time, but those early years of building Four-D Success Academy were like small seeds of faith being planted in the vineyard toward education and training for those that wanted it.

- The darkness of death is enough to stop you in your tracks. I am so grateful for the medical insight and knowledge that I have obtained. And when I'm facing the death of a loved one, I'm even more grateful for my trust in the Lord to keep me strong and purposeful, with an innate ability to demonstrate His love during the most difficult of times.

- As the business began to take shape, it was imperative that I kept my finger on the pulse of every area of my life. I am always balancing family, work, and faith. My prayer is that I am successful at doing so for as long as I desire to do so.

- I could not allow unexpected circumstances or other people's attitudes to hinder my forward progress. It is always important that I remain focused on my goals. Nor could I be afraid to reassess my immediate objectives. Change and flexibility are not always easy to embrace, but they become necessary as the vision continues to take shape.

- To run a business successfully requires one to be committed, and dedicated to the tasks before you. And, it's important that you don't become overwhelmed with all the planning, processes, and procedures that you must get acclimated to. You simply learn the rules of the business and apply yourself accordingly.

- My faith is a daily walk of expecting God to work everything out for my good! I think the thought, and in just a matter of time He manifests just what I need. His faithfulness to me overwhelms me to tears.

- Baby steps of faith. I work through the wisdom and strength of the Lord every single day!

- It is so important to keep positive people around you that believe in the hopes and dreams you have for yourself. So that when moments of uncertainty creep in, they are there to keep your eyes on the bigger picture.

- I can never be too busy or caught up in my own world to not consider others during their time of need.

- I never have to accept the word **_no_** as a final answer!

- The Lord will work through people to get you where He desires you to be. We should not ever put off for tomorrow what we are impressed to do right now. Stay in the moment and be obedient to His promptings.

- No matter what it looks like, we should always remain grateful, the best is yet to come!

- Hustle and flow… Always keep up with the demands of business as best you can!

- It is so important to stay within the timing of God, and not try to make things happen in your own timing, wisdom, or strength. He knows how to align everything in our favor.

- As the Founder and CEO, I must always keep an eye on the entire operation, even when there are people assigned to manage a particular department. Ultimately, it is my overall vision, expectations, and business that will be ill affected by poor employee performance if not realized in time. Consistent accountability will help to curtail surprises.

- Faith and love for God is the only sure foundation.

In a three-year timeframe and without any formal business education, I successfully launched a Training Institute that I know, beyond any doubt, God Himself called me to. Through strict obedience to the direction I received from the Lord, I have been able to pour into the lives of many, and to my soul's delight, I continue doing so 'til this day. While the journey has been vigorous and at times strenuous, I still have passion at my back, pushing me into what only God knows awaits me – much of which has been chronicled in the next journal.

Business by Faith

Journal 2

Begins: August 1, 1994 ~ 7:45 p.m.

Ends: December 10, 1996 ~ 6:55 p.m.

8/1/94 ~ 7:45 p.m.

Today the Riverside class started with 18 students. The new site is spacious. Shirley loves it.

We (Charlie and I) met with Brooker KCTV to discuss commercials. This will be a great marketing tool for the school. There is much to do. Today, Riverside notified us that the contract must be signed this week.

God is good...all the time. Enclosed is the 'new' brochure with INC.

8/9/94 ~ 5:03 p.m.

I signed the Riverside Contract for $272,000 on August 3rd. I put the class on hold until today.

I have been working on the commercial slated for August 23rd. The staff is busily working. The Acute Class has a new instructor Tonya Harrington.

God, as always, guides us. I pray for insight into the Colton site and the LVN Program. We are submitting a written request to contract with Hughes. This would be great! I hope and I pray to become more productive and efficient. We are going to be busy this year. It's important that we keep organized.

8/24/94

Much has happened. There have been times of concern/worry. Some fear of how I am going to keep things going. I turn to God. This past Sunday, I asked the Lord to give me a message and He did. He is my ROCK! On Sunday, I attended Loveland at 8:00 a.m. and Church of The Living God 11:00 p.m. services. Both ministries talked about going to the Rock. When in trouble, go the Rock. I was prayed for and I felt a release come from me and the tears flowed.

I received the answers to my question. God is my ROCK. He guides me, protects me from Satan and his actual workers, He pays all my bills, my rent, my staff. God speaks to me. I know it with all my heart.

It is now time for us to move. God will fill our seats with students and will fill our accounts with the funds. He will fill our minds with good word and He will open our mouths to speak His name, to share and witness to others His goodness. God is good and His mercy is everlasting.

I walk by faith. I live to be a servant of God, to serve Him through my love to help others. I feel joyful. I feel full. I feel peaceful. I am happy.

Thank You, God.

Last night, I added up deposits, YTD in all accounts. My Lord, $314,000 deposited. That's nothing but the Lord!

9/4/94 ~ 12:15

SEIZE THE MOMENT:

To think good thoughts

To be kind to others

To say positive words to another

To smile

To share your goodness

To spread the Word

To be thankful

To thank God for allowing you to walk in the land of the living.

Linda L. Smith

9/6/94 ~ 6:50 p.m.

Back from vacation. It was Hot-High 117 degrees. I found solitude in prayer and song. I had a talk with God. There is so much in my heart, I can't express. I fill with tears when I stop to say, "Thank You".

My mind seems to overflow with ideas and things to do. Sometimes I question if I am capable of operating this business as it grows, and then I remember God is operating this business and my fears leave, my smile returns, and peace sets in.

Pam had a baby boy on 9/2/94 at 12:30 p.m. Kaylen Jackson. Today, Cherry received the official notice from the BRN for Directorship for the LVN Program. I am awaiting the approval on the bid submitted for the Colton site. This is expected to move, grow, and show.

God, thank You.

We made a T.V. commercial on 8/22/94. Tomorrow, I will review it.

On August 26th at 9:30 a.m., my father had open-heart surgery. Replacement of the aortic valve and a quadruple bypass. He was discharged home on September 2nd (after 1 week) feeling pretty good. I am so thankful to God for his life and his ability to continue to show his words of love, kindness, and joy of living.

9/26/94 ~ 9:40 a.m.

Much has happened since my last entry. On Wednesday September 7th, Daddy was a little ill. He had not been eating (trying to lose weight) and was taking his meds incorrectly. I didn't suspect any problems. He had no unusual symptoms other than a small emesis after eating Jell-O. His headache seemed associated with his surgery. His perspiration occurred after his emesis. He slept well that night. On September 8th, I was paged. My father had been taken to S.B. Community Hospital ER. He was in serious condition. The ER nurse Suzanne, God Bless her, worked on Daddy and prayed for him. Daddy stayed at the Hospital until Friday afternoon and then he was transferred to Kaiser Sunset. I remained by his side from Thursday through Saturday night. He had 1500 cc fluid drained from around his heart and 400 cc from his thoracic cavity. He never complained. He talked, laughed, and prayed. I know God was with us. I went home Sunday afternoon on the 11th after he was transferred out of ICU. I can see him clear in my mind, looking out of the window, staring into the clear sky. My father had peace; he had no fear. I kissed him goodbye for the last time.

On Monday at 6:50 a.m., I jumped from my bed with urgency to call and inquire about my father. I reached for my purse, retrieved the phone number, and dialed. "Hello, this is Linda Smith. I am calling to see how my father, Walter Russ is doing."

A calm voice on the other end, "We are in an emergency right now. Can you call back in 15 minutes?"

A sense of calmness filled me I envisioned the ER caring for my father. I could see the nursing unit in my mind's eye. I could see the floor plan; could they be working in his room? I could not wish this on another. I could see the faces of the other family members with anguish on their faces, worrying about their loved ones. The wife of the 75-year-old, the son of the mother, the mother, husbands, daughters, all of patients like my father. Only I didn't know if they knew Jesus like I did. Did they have a spiritual relationship with

Him? Did their loved one love Him as my father did? Filled with peace, I know the emergency nurse was referring to my father's condition!

I called the hospital back at 7:15. A doctor was on the phone. I knew the outcome, but I needed to hear it. He said, "We tried but we couldn't get his heart to stay pumping. We even opened up the chest and did manual stimulation. His heart just could not make it."

I instantly filled with sorrow, I cried, I screamed for my father, a man I loved. Ernell drove me to the hospital to say goodbye to him. My sister, Roshonn, arrived later with her mother.

Knowing he has peace, love, and joy in being in the presence of the Lord gives me peace. On Friday the 16th, while showering and crying, I began to praise the Lord for His goodness, His love, and His grace. I thanked Him for giving me a father such as Walter Russ. I thanked Him for filling him with peace. Suddenly I was filled with joy, for I knew if he had to come this way again, even to see me, he wouldn't. That brings me joy. I know where my father is. I know God is pleased with his life, his commitment to family, Church, and prayer. He was not a perfect man, but he loved the Lord, his Church, his minister, and his family. He gave me much. He was my father, my counselor, my consultant, my prayer partner, and my friend. I will miss his physical presence, but I know he lives within me. I ask God to allow our spirits to stay in touch. Daddy, I love you. Peace be with you, and let it multiply.

Love your daughter, Linda.

Daddy was buried on his Birthday September 20th 1994 at Pioneer Memorial Park. Services were held at Temple Baptist Church.

I will always cry tears of joy for you!

10/18/94 ~ 6:35 p.m.

It seems so long ago that I wrote in this book. Today, I am filled with painful emotions of conflict and confusion. I sit here at 8:25 a.m. crying and praying, seeking both divine grace and love. Thankful for what He has given to me through Four-D Success. Thankful for the staff and students. Thankful for the people He has put in my path to help me.

I trust that He will provide a way, open closed doors, and clear the path of the road I must travel. Lord, bless the programs that are in place and those to come.

Lord, You know me, and my needs, my faults, sins, desires, hopes, and dreams. Keep the school in Your GRACE. Allow us to continue to help others.

There are times I feel so alone without my father, but then again I have YOU.

11/3/94 ~ 9:25 a.m.

This week, I've been filled with sorrow. I truly miss my dad.

My husband has expressed words and actions concerning my move to Colton, and concerns of financial stability. I know God provides. He guides me daily. Ernell is concerned about me failing and not being able to pay the rent when we move. His anger and behavior is beyond me. I dismiss him from my spirit, for he is draining me. I have prayed, cried to God to strengthen me and to guide me.

My mother is not speaking to me. I received a letter from a lawyer, requesting signature on a Quick Claim Deed on her house. My presence is "clouding" her life. How sad it is that she dislikes me. I am no longer welcome in her home. I will not sign off on the house. If any of my brothers were responsible enough to follow through on her business, in case of illness or death, I would not have any problems. But the history of five of the six sons warrants caution on my behalf. In the best interest of them, I will remain on the house.

I have been focused on marketing the commercial to be aired on cable. I will need to make some changes. The LVN Program is coming along. The hospital seems to have some concerns with our agreement. I pray to God Vickie and Karen find favor in FDSA and agree to allow us to use the facility. I must find another facility for additional coverage.

Lord, keep me focused, guide me. Wrap me in Your grace. I am never removed from God's power. I am a child of God and blessed by all He has to give. I deserve the best. I work for the best and I receive only the best. I pray God grants FDSA a two-year contract with Riverside & San Bernardino County. Thank You, Jesus...

11/11/94 ~ 10:40 a.m.

Heavenly Father, I thank You for Your grace and mercy. I delivered a gift of popcorn to the Riverside Management. While there, I was informed of the $2.5 million excess that must be spent by June 1995. My Lord, we could see an additional $133,770 by June (training 30 students). I have met with the planners and the Colton office, and things seem to be going well.

I met with Susan from the state two weeks ago to discuss the possibility of being part of an "incubation program" at Norton. Glenda extended our coverage at the Public Enterprise Center through September 1995. The Lord is good. Charlie has insisted on establishing a Financial Committee for FDSA. I met with Skip and Pastor Crawford —it's a go. The commercial is aired. I have made changes (revisions) for the upcoming week airtime.

Denise is developing the Financial P&P manual. Cherry is working on the revision of the School P&P Manual. Dawn is working on office operation and Pam is working on the estate. Instructors teaching. Me, all I can. I am so grateful to God. Today, Mary said she and the students prayed. Mary had a special request. This is a blessing. I pray that God shows me how to be of assistance to my staff and others. I pray that He shows me how to effectively communicate with Ernell regarding our children, needs, desires, and Four-D. I pray that my focus is not clouded with negativism. I pray for peace, understanding, guidance, patience, and love for others and myself. I pray for my mother. I pray for peace. She and I have not spoken since Daddy's funeral or shortly thereafter. I ask God to show me how to approach her, what to say, and what not to say. I pray for her health and happiness. I feel good today. Life is good, and there's much to do!

Heavenly Father, thank You, for who I am.

11/16/94 ~ 6:00 p.m.

I thank God for this day. I deposited $29,353 into the FDSA Account. Bills will be paid! I submitted a letter to Riverside JTPA for more students. God will provide. I received a call today from Pomona Urban League —seeking employment (OJT) contract. I will be in need of an Intake Assistant person with excellent communication, staff, and knowledge of computers. God is laying a new foundation for the future of Four-D Success Academy. I am seeking clinical agreements with Riverside General and with Loma Linda Hospital.

God, I ask for these sites. Through You, all things are possible. I claim victory in Your name. We will be successful and have a TOP-NOTCH LVN Program.

Show me how to increase the enrollment into the Acute Aide Training and Continue Ed. Classes.

He did.

- ✓ Do commercial specifically for above.
- ✓ Change Acute ad from 64 hours to 3 weeks.

Now let's see what happens, Thank You, Lord.

11/21/94 ~ 10:30

Job Connection is being aired. I, along with two students, participated in a 30-minute camera interview. I have received calls on how well we did. Four-D Success Academy will sponsor Job Connection for 1 year, starting January 1995.

Mike informed me of the contract being signed with the Colton site this week. God, I thank You for this blessing. Please guide us.

Rent is paid, salaries paid, bills paid - Thank You, Jesus. I continue to seek avenues to market at less cost. God is showing me how.

My mind is flooded!

11/27/94 ~ 10:20 p.m.

God, guide me through this day. I think of my Dad and cry. Today's message dealt with being content. Daddy was content. He appreciated all that God had given him. I ask God to protect Wilbert, Zack, and Greg while in prison. My brothers are so far removed from me. I didn't see momma on Thanksgiving, but I talked to her on the phone the day after. Silence is so painful. I thank Jesus for this day of life, joy, love, and the happiness I have. I am content.

11/28/94 ~ 11:10 a.m.

I just spoke with Vicki Lombardo at San Bernardino Community Hospital. She confirmed that the FDSA contract agreement will stand. Thank You, Jesus. The write up in the Sun Telegram is great. We will have 17 students.

12/15/94 ~ 2:35 p.m.

Yes! Riverside students are getting jobs. Four placed this week. No findings with Riverside/San Bernardino County Monitors.

Riverside contract will be expanded to $133,770 to train 33 and place 30 students.

Working on Colton site. Jesus is blessing us!

God provides the CNA's. The Word says, "Ask and it will be given; seek, ye shall find; knock, the door will be opened." Two days ago, the check balance showed $2,000. Yesterday, I deposited $31,000. Payroll and bills are paid. The Lord is good. Advertisement is going well. I was interviewed by the Precinct Reporter and Church and Community News and the Sun Telegram Papers. The commercial is being aired.

God, guide me, bring unto my door the help I need to continue my work in helping others. Let my desire to reach out always exceed the financial gain of all FDSA and I do.

Let my blessing be the success to reach others, touch their lives and make a difference, and to bathe in Your kind grace and the opportunities to minister.

I am eternally grateful to be selected for this work. Thank You, Lord, for the staff present and those to come.

The Lord will provide all of our needs. Through <u>unquestionable faith,</u> I stand firm in believing in His will that this work that we do is good.

Joy, joy, joy. How sweet Jesus is!

12/19/94 ~ 9:27 a.m.

I received a call from Mike Ballard regarding the Colton site. Things are good. They (landlord) are willing to allow us to pay $1,700 for the first two months. God is good. Lord, thank You.

Lydia Martinez called today. She's a FDSA graduate. This student is full of joy. She recently purchased a 1988 Cadillac in cash, and for the first time since 1985 she has a Christmas tree and presents for her kids. She represents what FDSA strives for. I am so thankful for this opportunity. Lord, thank You.

1/2/95 ~ 6:36 p.m.

A new year is upon us and we are with God. I have been at the Claremont office since 12 noon, cleaning up and enjoying the quiet and praying. I am so thankful to God to have completed another year with the school. We exceeded the requirements for placement with all three contracts, still waiting to hear from Riverside Extension with funds, and we're awaiting final contract for the Colton space. I am humbled by God's presence in my life. I am so grateful for His love for me. Four-D Success Academy, Inc. will have a prosperous 1995 in training and revenue.

I hired two full-time staff persons. One to assist with intake at the office starting 12/27/94, and the other a RN instructor to start Feb. 1995.

Cherry and I will travel to Sacramento to work on two projects: 1) Meet with Marcia Peterson about the LVN program, and 2) Seek out the area for new site and meet with Director. God will guide us and bless this trip.

My prayer for 1995: Dear Lord, grant us the opportunity to help others through our endeavors. Let us do this work with full devotion and love for You. Keep us focused on our mission. Keep us humble in Your presence. Show us how to better ourselves. Fill us with joy and happiness. Keep us loving towards all humanity.

Let 1995 be fulfilled with hundreds of graduates who will love the opportunity to pray with us. Let us make a difference in someone's life.

God, thank You for giving me this opportunity. Allow me to please carry on.

Your Child, Linda

Daddy, I miss you terribly. I know you are watching over me with Jesus. Keep praying and smiling. Love you, Linda

1/9/95

There are days I feel on top of the world and there are days like this when I feel lower or in a daze. We're seeking beds, waiting on news with Riverside Contract and Colton Site.

Jesus, I call on Your name.

Carry me through the difficult times ahead. You will not forsake me!

Linda L. Smith

Thank You.

1/16/95 ~ 2:00 p.m.

Although I feel an emotional burden, I give thanks to God for what He has given me. Dawn is doing fine post-surgery. I do miss her.

The new hire, Joanne Williams, quit after 2 weeks. The Lord knows what we can handle and He will provide someone who will blend in perfectly. I submitted the signed contract with a check to Mike Ballard. The Colton site is coming.

God is blessing us with the Riverside Contract. Year end will be $405,770. Students are graduating and getting jobs. Lord, let me continue to stand. Provide a foundation where I can stand and say, "Through God, all things are possible."

I am so grateful to God for paying the bills.

Keep me Lord in Your GRACE.

Guide me through the darkness I am feeling within.

Forgive me when I fall.

1/21/95 ~ 10:35 a.m.

On January 20th, God sent FDSA a wonderful person to join our staff. I know Margie will be an asset to us. I met with Linda Stratton about the Colton site. Since our meeting, things seem to be moving ahead. I brought eight electrical beds yesterday! I was driving EAST on Central towards Waterman and, lo and behold, on a rainy day, were stacks of electrical beds. What a blessing from God.

We are going to be in the San Bernardino Black History Parade on 2/4 and the Riverside Parade on 2/14.

God is good, all the time.

Dawn is doing fine. Recovery is going well. I look forward to my New York trip with my fashion consultant Donna. She is a scream!

Since August 2, 1994 the deposit book shows $276,748.

God bless this day! Today, I receive the Women of Excellence Award!

2/5/95 ~ 11:50 a.m.

Feeling blue. My heart is heavy as I examine the events in my personal life. I miss my father terribly. My mother is the same. I turn to God for peace. Four-D is doing well. God blessed us with the extended funds of $133,770 from Riverside County.

I must now prepare for a Contract proposal. Cherry, Denise, and I have our work cut out for us. I know we will meet all deadlines. The staff continues to perform well.

Lord, guide me! Fill me with wisdom, patience, love, and understanding.

Lord, search my heart. Keep me in Your grace.

2/9/95 ~ 12:07 p.m.

Yesterday, I received a call from Robert Rochelle. He had two clients to refer. I had prayed for two! I signed the modification contract with Riverside for $405,770.

Life is good!

2/16/95 ~ 6:35 p.m.

I'm working on the San Bernardino County & Riverside County contracts. I rushed to meet the 2/21 deadline established by me. Contracts are due 2/27 & 3/2 respectfully.

I signed the contract for Colton site. Lord is with us, $5,422 a month!

At 7:00 a.m., Donna and I will be on a plane (1st class) to New York! Friday through Monday night.

Then I leave on Wednesday morning for San Francisco for an Accreditation Workshop until Saturday.

We move in March. Busy times ahead.

We all are working hard!

Heavenly Father, my Guide, I give You honor and praise. Thank You so much for all we have received thus far. I pray that You continue to guide us and keep us focused always. Let our prime concern and focus be on our students! Amen.

Your Grateful Child, Linda

I think of my father and smile.

2/26/95 ~ 11:30 p.m.

I sit here quietly, listening to soft music on the radio. I am so grateful to God for giving me this wonderful opportunity to do this work.

For the past two weeks, Cherry, Denise, and I have pushed to complete the Riverside and San Bernardino contracts proposed today.

San Bernardino is due by 5 p.m. on February 27th (tomorrow!). And Riverside is due March 3rd by 5.p.m. We are submitting a CNA and LVN Proposal to both Counties. God be with us.

We received the additional $133,770 for Riverside. Tomorrow, 16 of the 30 students will start. The Intake team has done a wonderful job.

I attended an Accreditation Workshop in San Francisco last week. It was held February 22nd-25th. In order to apply, we would need to put the LVN Program on hold. Well, I guess accreditation will have to wait.

Heavenly Father, I pray and ask that You guide the heart of our state consultant. I pray she acts favorably towards us. Enable the LVN Program to start timely. Continue to keep FDSA in Your grace and protection.

Thank You so much for the new Colton site. Grant us the funds needed to operate and grow. Guide me and the staff. Allow us to always be professional, ethical, kind, generous at heart, and God-filled.

Thank you. Ladies, thanks for rising to the occasion and responding professionally. Love, Linda

I went to New York with Donna, February 16th-20th. What a trip. What a city. Thanks, Donna, for your lovely generosity and friendship.

Where can we go next!

3/3/95 ~ 4:50 p.m.

Today, I got on my knees and asked God for help. Help me to make the best judgment call as a manager and send me help. Enable me to

115

let go and use (delegate to) staff.

My prayers were answered in the staff meeting.

Cherry - placement specialist.

Sharon - request attendance to workshop.

Adenia - attend workshop in Tahoe.

Pam - great input on Placement System.

Let go, let God, and let staff.

I have journeyed from "I" to "We" this day.

I am relieved.

Thank You, Jesus.

3/14/95 ~ 8:50 a.m.

Moving right along. Phones have been selected for the new site and the furniture is being purchased. I received a call from JTPA about Placement Services. They questioned if we were placing students. Several had said we had not placed them. I held an emergency meeting with the staff. The issues were addressed. There is much to do!

Lord, help me organize! We need sound systems.

Considering Non-Profit status entity. Thank You, Jesus for this day.

3/17/95 ~ 7:05 a.m.

I want to take time to write a note to thank the Lord for the blessings He continues to bestow upon Four-D Success Academy. The Colton site is coming along. Each visit is a wonderment of how this all came about. I thank God for His grace and guidance.

The checkbook is low. But checks continue to come in. That's God. He knows when the bills are due. We at Four-D simply work for them!

Today, I am going to visit Wilbert. God, grant me a safe trip. Keep my family, friends, and strangers in Your loving embrace.

Continue to guide me, Lord. Help me become a better manager for the school. Thank You for the people You have placed in my life and the path I have traveled to get to this point.

Bless this day with Your presence.

3/28/95 ~ 8:30 a.m.

I stood in the receptionist area and shed a tear. We are moving. The certificates and bulletin boards are off the wall.

The Colton site is coming. God has granted us a beautiful building.

He is directing our path. We follow His lead.

I think of many things and smile. On Saturday, I spoke to a group at the hospice "Festival of Love" in Victorville. It's nice to participate actively and be a part of something good.

I feel good today. God is Love.

4/3/95 ~ 10:20 a.m.

Today, we move to Colton. Things are packed. I arrived at 6:45 a.m. I prayed to God for the blessings He has given us. I prayed for His love, guidance, financial support, for teamwork, and team effort. I prayed for the opportunities to help others and open doors. I prayed for personal accomplishment of each staff member. I ask that He

117

continue to send knowledgeable, spiritual, caring individuals who support the purpose for which we exist.

This is truly an emotional period for me. Things are moving in my life. I let go of Daddy's things. I need to close another door. I visited his gravesite and I know he is wherever I am and with me spiritually. Yesterday in Church, I became full with God's presence. I prayed for my brothers, mother, family, school, staff, everything. Sometimes I am heavily burdened. I know God will carry me through.

I await the outcome of our proposal. God has blessed us with His anointed hand. We have work to do. I have requested focus and endurance to continue to do the work He has appointed me to. I submit unto His will.

We moved into this place on August 3, 1992.

We moved out on April 3, 1995.

I smile. I thank God.

1994-1995 is a good year for Four-D Success Academy, Inc.

I will apply for a non-profit status within the next four weeks.

Thank You, Heavenly Father, for Your love, grace, and mercy.

Your child, Linda

4/4/95 ~ 7:50 a.m.

What a day it was. The movers from San Bernardino & El Monte had things delivered by 2:30 p.m. The movers from Claremont started at 11 a.m. and ended at 12:45 a.m. I will never know why it took three men so long to move out of the office. But thank God, it's done.

The new site is great! I'm so grateful to God for it.

Today, the ladies and I are going to clean everything up and put them away. This is going to be a busy month for me. I have trips to Sacramento, Newport Beach, South Tahoe and LA for audits, monitoring, you name it. We've got to do it.

Thank You, Lord, my Heavenly Father.

4/5/95 ~ 6:05 p.m.

Today is a blessed day. I was able to purchase office furniture at a great price. My office has cherry wood chairs. Things are coming together.

Today, I met Evelyn Harper. She's graduating from New York Regis BS Program and is seeking clinical proctors. We may have a new program here!

Everyone is pleased with our new site. Our Open House is going to be great. I look forward to a brighter future.

4/12/95 ~ 6:20 p.m.

Yesterday, Cherry and I flew to Sacramento to meet with LVN State Consultant. The meeting went well overall but we have changes to make. We have much to do: test, Policy & Procedures, etc.. But 9/7/95 to start seems very possible. The goal is to be fully prepared for the Board meeting on 7/1/95.

Driving to work today, I thought of how fortunate we are. I am glad we put in for the LVN Program with the County proposal. Then my pager goes off with a 911 to call the office. Riverside JTPA approved the 112 CNA students @ $4,000 for $448,000 and the LVN for first year $165,000 for 15 students. I screamed and cried. God is good.

119

The checkbook showed $252 yesterday. I have since written a check for $144. Today, I got a call that the Riverside check is in the mail for $39,000. We had 17 students in the Cont. Ed class on Saturday, and five students in the evening HHA Class.

We are going to outgrow this building in one year (in my heart) or two years (in my mind). Today, I closed the SB storage. I gave away the last items belonging to my father to a young man who truly appreciated them. Daddy, I'm full of joy, laughter, tears, and sorrow. I miss you deeply but I know if we could speak to one another you would say how proud you are of me. Love you much.

Jesus, thank You for this blessed day.

4/15/95 ~ 9:55 a.m.

Yesterday, we had our first staff meeting. All were there. It was nice to have everyone present. We all are so grateful to God to have our new building. He continues to guide us as we follow.

I feel a tremendous spirit of calmness. Several weeks ago, I was told my taxes would be $48,000. I almost freaked. Yesterday, I was told they were $64,239. I was calm. I know that God will take care of His will. Four-D Success is waiting on checks now! Denise and I are holding our payroll checks to avoid things from bouncing (since 4/7/95). I checked our balance. It states $34,000. I guess someone is holding out, buying time, or I have made another mathematical error of $20,000. The Lord knows my heart, only He and He alone. I know my Father Walter is proud of me. Thank You, Jesus, Linda & Staff

4/21/95

On 4/17/95, God enabled FDSA, Inc. to pay all of its taxes — $64,000 plus. All of our bills are paid and on the 18th we received the Riverside check. I am so grateful to God for His blessing.

I feel like I have not been focused to my fullest. I will dedicate my time next week to completing all minor tasks and addressing major issues.

Thank You, Lord.

5/1/95 ~ 6:55 p.m.

Several days ago, I was asked to write a book. Although I laughed at the idea, I indicated I had been asked several years ago to do the very same thing. This student felt my story would inspire others. The title of the book will be "You are My Success." The YOUS are: The I AM (God), students, family, individuals I meet, and friends. One day.

Adenia, Cherry, and I attended a good workshop put on by CACHE in Tahoe. There's lots of work to do. The 1st Advisory meeting was held 4/28/95. Good Team, E. Carrillo, Ms. Barfield, Mary Ann Payne, Charlie Seymour, Cherry Houston, Dawn Gaines (sect), and me. Lots of work to do. Financially, things are stable. God blessed the Continued Education Class with 17 students on Saturday 4/29/95.

Lord, keep me focused and productive. Enable me to make wise choices and decisions. Keep FDSA and me on the lighted path.

Many times, I think of my father. Oh how I miss him so. He fulfilled the spiritual, emotional, and communication needs in my life. I didn't realize how much we shared and how much he gave me peace until he was gone. I truly appreciated his presence. Our relationship was special. He guided me, counseled me, embraced me, kissed me, and loved me, all as a father. So many days have I been down. I know God lifts me, but the absence of Daddy from my life allows me to see my life clearly and the many voids he filled. I pray to God for understanding, guidance, and peace in my life, feelings, and actions.

I sit here at the new site. The air is still, interrupted by occasional creeping, settling sounds of the walls. I am relieved, quiet, and calm. There is much to do. Yet I feel peace at this time. No rush, no anxiety, no pain — as though Daddy was sitting across from me here in my office. I look at his picture and at his smile, and I know all is all right. I can hear him saying, "The Lord is going to work everything out."

Daddy, I Love You, Your Girl, Linda

5/4/95 ~ 4:55 p.m.

I received a call from Felicia Miller from Riverside County about monitoring of programs. Excellent report. Only one finding regarding the Individual Student Service Plan. She will mail the sample for our use.

I received a letter from SB County, approval for CNA @ $4,000 each and LVN @ $11,000 each. Lord, this is great.

I interviewed Delores Turner for a position. She truly would be an asset to FDSA. We're negotiating the salary. Things will work out.

Signs are being made for the building. The pictures are hung in the Conference Room and lobby. Beautiful!

I received a call from San Antonio. Hal Wadell has supplies and equipment to donate to us.

Received a call from Renden. Adam hired four FDSA students. They are very pleased with appearance and performance.

I will submit non-profit in 1-2 weeks. God is good, all the time.

Received an extension for Riverside & San Bernardino CNA until 6/97. I am smiling. I'm extremely happy.

5/10/95 ~ 9 a.m.

This morning I felt anxious. I was feeling the need to get things done and go to the Riverside site and talk with students. Then I stood still and sought calmness. I spoke with Sharon at Riverside. She handled the issues with the students.

On my way to work, I prayed for calmness and peace. I asked God to help me be a better manager of people and show me what I needed to do to get the job done, to tell me what to do today. I prayed that I would listen and respond. He knows our financial status, our students' status, and our staffing status. He knows everything and He will take care of all things.

I arrived to work. The ladies are busy typing and the form for the copier is done. Adenia gave a gift of Dutch Apple Tea (25 bags). The box was sitting on my desk, and seeing the note lifted my spirits instantly.

I noted where another sign should go on the building for easier identification. I spoke with N. Finch, RN at State regarding Home Health Aide program. Renewal notice sent 4/28. We will receive renewal. Thanks, God! We have 32 students scheduled to graduate Friday the 12th at our new site. Lord, this is great. I pray that each will strive to do their best in life. I pray that they will take what we have given them and improve upon the situations of their lives. I know we have been able to help someone, and that alone is all I ask. Let me make a difference in someone's life. Let me stand and say, "Through God, all things are possible." I am at PEACE.

Thank You, Jesus. Your Child, Linda

5/12/95 ~ 6:10 p.m.

What a blessed day! Today, 32 ladies graduated. What a wonderful program. Guest speakers were Tahira Smith, Robert Rochelle, and M. Martinez. We had 75 plus guests.

I attended Community Convalescent Hospital's Open House, and set off my alarm at the facility. What a day, what a day!

God is good, all the time. I know my daddy is proud of me.

I am so grateful to the staff for their support.

Thanks, Lord, for this day!

5/25/95

We received 2 calls from San Bernardino County for referrals for the LVN Program. One interview was held, the other to come. Cherry is truly turning out the papers. I am so excited!

The HHA Day class has 10+ students. Riverside has 17 students.

The Open House will be great. It will be from 4-7 p.m. Lord, so much is coming and You are helping us to meet all deadlines.

I became a member of the Advisory Board to SB County PIC, a Board Member of the Inland Empire Community Health Center, and MT. View Com, Inc. Hospice. And today, we obtained our Non-Profit

Status. Name of the Co.: Friends of Four-D Success Academy.

All is well. I am happy.

I am so grateful to God for this blessing — to give back, to provide opportunity, to grow, to love freely, and to be happy.

Thank You, Lord.

6/1/95 ~ 6:10 p.m.

Sunday, Charlie and Al put up our sign. It looks great! We are planning for the Open House. There is much to do before 6/15, but we will be ready.

God guides us each day. I pray for peace, patience, focus, productivity, support to the staff. This Saturday, we are going to a "dressy" affair. We will have fun. God is good, all the time. Tomorrow, I'll go see Wilbert.

6/5/95 ~ 6:35 p.m.

God is good. Although I had to release a staff member today, I know God will replace her. We are working towards the Open House. The facility looks good. I must spend a day here alone. Maybe Saturday — to write, think, and pray. I do thank God daily, but it's nice to have quiet prayer time. The Church Temple wishes to establish a scholarship fund in my father's name! I will donate $200. Lord, guide each of us, enable us to be our very best.

Thank You for paying the bills!

6/7/95 ~ 7:03 p.m.

Oh, what a blessed day. I reviewed the contract with Loren; we need to make some adjustments. I am excited and stimulated with the need to accomplish goals by 6/30. I had a wonderful visit with Pastor

Dowdy. The staff is truly working to meet and exceed expectations. I am pleased! I think of my dad often. I wonder if my mother will attend the Open House. The caterers, the harpist, news coverage, invitations are all are covered. I've been told I need a new chair. This is my least concern. In fact, this is a step above what I had. This one has screws holding it together. So funny. ☺ I will write a letter to Sadiq now.

6/11/95 ~ 9:35 a.m.

On this Sunday, I am at the office, not so much to work but to be alone and thank God. I drove up and became filled with His presence. I am really here by God's grace. The front door says "Entrance," the window display is the lamp logo. Oh how beautiful it is. I enter to my place of peace. Not my place — this building — but a place in my heart and my spirit where I go for peace. I look around, walk the halls, look at the pictures, the furniture, the equipment, and I know HIM. I know I work for Him. I know that all of this belongs to Him. I am so graceful that He allows me to work for HIM.

I kneel and pray. I thank Him, I praise Him, I cry for Him. I know He knows me like no other. He knows my heart, my mind, my desire, and He knows me. He guides me and provides peace for me, and protects me. He pays all of our bills. He enables us to obtain contracts. He is just blessing the LVN Program.

Marcia Peterson is going on vacation, but as the Lord would have it, she has scheduled FDSA, Inc. to be presented to the LVN Board on July 15th.

I know He will see this through. I requested a two-year contract for the LVN Program with Riverside. We were approved for $165,000 for

12 months but the program is 14 months. LVN wishes to train 30 students over a two-year period. It will be granted!

Lord, I thank You.

The Open House is set for June 15th. It will be blessed and grand! I am so excited. He has taken me to this. I am humbled and I am thankful. It is wonderfully quiet, only the ticking of the clock.

Lord, thank You. Michelle and my daddy would love to see this place. I miss both of you so much.

6/12/95 ~ 6:15 p.m.

Worked with Loren on LVN contract possibly for 15-30 students. No guarantee on enrollees. Lord, I walk by faith. I know He will guide us.

I received a 'thank you' from a grad of CNA Program. She is working and happy. Lord, guide us, protect us, and enable us to do more for others.

6/14/95 ~ 4:10 p.m.

Today, I signed off on the CNA Riverside Contract for $448,000. Driving away from the building, I yelled, "My God, $448,000!" Three years ago, 6/92, I was nervously waiting to hear from San Bernardino County for my first contract. We started with two students. Today, I signed to train 112 students for Riverside alone.

God, I feel great. Tomorrow is our Open House and my baby Aisha will be 17 years old. What a joy!

Each day, I learn something new. Today, I corrected an error in a management decision I made. I reassigned titles without considering the impact on staff involved. I am grateful to God for

His blessing and wisdom. Lord, I am filled with tears and joy. I give all honor to You. I thank You from the depth of my heart and soul for this unselfish blessing You have bestowed upon Four-D Success Academy, Inc.

I can't write all I feel, but You know all of my thoughts, feelings, fears, joy, and triumphs to come. This building looks great! I called my mother to see if she was coming. She's not. One grandson with chicken pox and she's having her house painted. She brings such sorrow to my heart. Nevertheless, I pray for a wonderful turnout. We have worked hard to get here. Lord, bless us please!

Your Loving Child, Linda

6/15/95 ~ 3:33 p.m.

Today is the day! Open House is here. I am nervous. Lord, bless this day. Loren from Riverside County called. The LVN Contract is ready. Today, I sign. Thank You, Jesus.

I look out the window and I see cars passing. Lord, let them come our way. I need to do last-minute checks.

6/15/95 ~ 7:55 p.m.

Well, the day has come to an end. The Open House was successful. Thank You, Jesus. The caterer did an excellent job. The harpist was lovely. Shirley's daughter, Kim, sung two beautiful songs. The guests enjoyed the environment. Such an exciting day and blessed event.

I am so fortunate to have such a wonderful, supportive staff. I love them all. Thank You, Jesus.

6/17/95 ~ 7:15 p.m.

I attended the first session of the last class to clear Teaching Credential.

Yesterday, the checking account dropped below $5,000. By the time staff went to cash their checks, the bank indicated "not enough funds." I had begun the process of transferring $25,000 to account. I thank God for the availability to the line of credit. Today, the Riverside check for $45,028.75 arrived. God is good.

I received the San Bernardino Contracts for S.R. Contracts. CNA $4,000 and LVN $11,000.

I must complete P&P and information for Council by Tuesday the 20th.

Oh Happy Day!

6/23/95 ~ 6:50 p.m.

The end of another busy day, and we're going in the right direction. Each staff member is fully doing their job. I am pleased. We have so much to be thankful for. For God is good. All the time.

The Riverside site is coming along beautifully with the remodeling. Shirley will be so pleased.

Lord, enable me to continue to help others.

7/12/95 ~ 3:35 p.m.

Today is my 20th anniversary. It's been a long haul, but we made it. I am not as joyful as I hoped to be. So much has touched my spiritual and emotion frame, to the point that I feel numb. God has kept us together.

There is joy in knowing my (our) daughters have a home with two parents. They are adjusted, loved, and supported. The quality of life is not guaranteed. We only strive to improve and maintain what we have.

I am grateful to God! The business is going well, we may not have to pay taxes on Corp. and we may be able to issue a small bonus to staff.

We will start the year off with two classes of CNA next week!

God is good.

1995-96 is going to be an explosive year for Four-D Success Academy, Inc.

Thank You, Jesus.

7/17/95 ~ 4:56 p.m.

I enjoyed Las Vegas. I saw two shows: Spellbound and Mystri.

I feel blue today. So much energy spent on advertising and marketing and referring clients to San Bernardino JTPA County and received only two referrals for class, which starts 7/24/95. Both referrals are from Robert Rochelle. I know we are in God's care. I wish we had more students to help. The Nursing State Consultant put our program on hold. She wants some changes made. Cherry has an appointment on the 24th to meet with her. Lord, touch her heart! Make a way for FDSA. Enable us to start the LVN class in September, and no later than November.

Lord, keep me focused! Show me where to go! Open up doors for me to enter.

7/31/95 ~ 3:30 p.m.

I must take a minute to STOP and give <u>written</u> thanks to God for all of His many wonderful blessings.

We started our year with 23 students. Riverside – 20; San Bernardino County – 1; City – 1.

We will offer our first RNA program on August 22nd and 23rd.

The LVN application process is going well. Cherry has done an excellent job. I know it will be accepted by the State Consultant for the September Board Meeting. We are getting a lot of referrals.

Friends of Four-D Success Academy Non-Profit had its first meeting on July 27, 1995!

I requested Mary Ann Payne as Chairperson, Denise Champion as Treasurer, and Cherry Houston as Secretary. I am President and Ernell is Vice President, as the Executive Committee. I wish to obtain funds for Ed/Training (my minds jumping). I also wish to obtain a vehicle for transporting students and establish a Child Care Center.

I placed an ad in "Attention Nurses" and the person I was speaking to informed me of an owner in Long Beach who wished to sell her school. I have an appointment on 8/4 at 11:00 a.m. to meet her at her home. If this is good, then God will open the door.

The Home Health Aide and Acute Aide program is low. I will continue to strive to increase enrollment.

If there were one thing I could ask of the Lord, it would be to let me continue to LOVE my work, for it (my work) affects every aspect of my life. It comforts me.

I think of my dad often and cry. Not profusely as before and my heart doesn't ache as bad. I often think about what he would say or do, and I am able to get through the day.

Jesus, thank You for all.

8/9/95 ~ 1:30

On August 7th, I turned 43. My mind is so matted with thoughts. I am unclear as to my next step. I ask God to guide me.

San Bernardino Community Hospital says they can't find any contracts with the hospital, which were signed months ago.

I know God is with me and He guides me. My path is life. I must not become discouraged.

Lord, steady my heart.

8/15/95

I know He guides me. I will try to obtain a facility agreement with Bixby Knoll Towers in Long Beach. I feel guided by the Lord. I thank Him so much.

We are working a new marketing angle. We're mailing it to all our students. Lord let this be successful, increase our private dollars.

Today, my braces came off. What a lovely bright SMILE!

I met with Rosalyn from San Bernardino Community Hospital. She could not find a thing on us! I took over copies for resubmission.

Ontario JTPA office continues to be non-supportive of FDSA. Receiving calls from clients stating they are being discouraged from attending here, that funds are not available. I request Colton Office clarify our status with the Ontario Office. I chose not to submit a grievance and will not deal with the negativity. Four-D Success Academy will keep its door open...God is good! All the time!

9/1/95

It doesn't seem that long ago that I wrote in this book, but time does go on! Well, I did meet with the Bixby Knolls DON & DSD. I presented FDSA, our desires and objectives of our program. I left the Facility Agreement for signature. Each lady indicated the desire to work with us. We mailed applications and requested resumes. God guides this path.

Three students in Riverside were suspended for stealing and for participating in the act. I will make a decision Tuesday of final outcome.

The submission of papers to the consultant for the VN Program is complete. We await the consultant.

Today, Shirley Howard and I spoke. She sees FDSA occupying this entire complex! Let the Lord lead us.

The year of my father's death is approaching. September 12th will be one year. I think of him daily. When I'm down, or need focus I look at his picture and think 'What would Daddy say?' He never steered me wrong and he used God in his walk. I know the Lord is carrying my family, the school, the staff, and me. I am so grateful to His very presence and love for me.

I am here alone. It's quiet, except for the clock ticking softly in the background. My mind is clear, I feel at ease. I feel God's presence. I have peace.

I know all that FDSA will do, will be done through, by, and for God. All bills will be paid, the classrooms will be filled, and highly qualified staff will fill needed positions.

The Lord has always come before on time, and He is here now.

The Lord is my Shepherd, I shall not want.

He provides all my needs.

Thank You, Heavenly Father, for giving me what no person could give me on this Earth: PEACE.

Love You.

As I sit and look out of the half-closed blinds, I think of what He has done for me.

9/11/95 ~ 8:25 a.m.

Cherry has written and rewritten the Vocational Nurse Program according to the instructions of Marcia Peterson. Yesterday, I felt the strong urgency to call her and ask that she find favor in FDSA. The objectives have been met. Lord, touch her heart, her presentation, her mind. You have laid the foundation for us to move forward. I know Satan wishes to block our path but I stand firm in believing that through You, all things are possible. As I place this call to Marcia today, I pray You control the thoughts I think, the words I speak, and that she is attentive to me. Well, she said, "Not all is lost." She needs the total package, which she knows Cherry is sending overnight to her. She is going to meet with her supervisor to review our program. The format is looking good and she intends on presenting it to the new board.

Lord, I ask in Your name to conclude this in favor of FDSA. I thank You so much for Cherry – her endless hours of dedication and labor of love. I am overwhelmed with emotions of joy. I know You will provide. I can't doubt You! Last week, the checking account was $6,000. Payday was on Friday, but Thursday, my Lord delivered $69,000+ to us. All bills were paid, plus we had $5,000 left over. Oh, what a mighty good God I serve.

Tomorrow is my daddy's one-year anniversary of his going home to the Lord. Although I miss him, in times like this, I look at his picture and I hear his words of trust in God and faith. I know, I know, I KNOW everything is ALL RIGHT.

I have no doubt, no sadness. I feel calm, peace, and joy.

Thanks, Lord.

9/18/95 ~ 2:25

Last week was an emotional week for me. On 9/12/94, Daddy died. It's been a year since his death. I miss him so much. San Bernardino Community Hospital reneged on our facility agreement for the LVN Program, and refused to sign the CNA agreement.

Saint B's is still open. Final signature sought. We have been contacted by a young lady who works for the Job Corp. There may be work for us there.

I will resubmit for the HHA Program for LA County and Long Beach.

There is, as always, much to do. God, keep me focused and guide me.

Sincerely, Linda

9/21/95 ~ 5:40 p.m.

Yesterday was Daddy's day of birth. I know where he is. I truly do miss him! Today, St. B's indicated we would receive a facility agreement for the LVN Program.

God is with us.

We are preparing for the upcoming classes in October. Things are going well. Sometimes, the checkbook is in the negative, BUT I know God will pay ALL bills.

Have a great day.

9/27/95 ~ 11:00

I feel numb. Today, Ernell, Aisha, and I went to family counseling. I don't know what is going to happen to us. We, as a family, may not exist in the future. There is much heartache, pain, and loneliness. I feel anger in my heart. Twenty years, and I feel full. Lord, help me.

Marcia Peterson – Consultant says the VN Program will not be presented until Jan 26, 1996. Minor adjustment. I just don't know how she supports or feels about FDSA. We are anxious and ready. Yet, she finds fault. Maybe it's me and my desire, our desire, to establish this program and become a visible alternative in this area. God, be with us.

Lord, keep me focused, give me encouragement, and guidance.

Sadness is a horrible feeling.

Love, Linda…Lord, lift me up!

10/9/95 ~ 2:55 p.m.

Today, I received good news. San Bernardino Community Hospital will reinstate our programs. When I received the denial in August, I asked God for help. I called Nancy Sedlack and left a message on her phone. She has inside contacts. I then waited. Last week, God woke me up and instructed me to write a letter to Karen Price, V.P. Clinical services. So I did. Today she called and asked what I needed. I requested reinstatement for the CNA Program and access for the future LVN Students. I will resubmit all contract and insurance papers today.

- ✓ Transworld is working on defaults.
- ✓ The Educational Financial Success pack will be submitted this week.
- ✓ God allowed us to make payroll on Friday.

I pray I stay faithful and trust in Him always. Doors that close, close only for a moment. Thank You, Lord.

10/10/1995

Today, I had lunch with Ted Holt, Adm. of Life Care Center of Corona. Will he ask Four-D to provide training to meet with the DSTS requirement of their survey? Well, we may have a contract. I delivered our contracts back (3x) to San Bernardino Community Hospital. I look forward to returning to the facility.

My Secretary, Dawn Grimes, informed me she is leaving in January 1996. I ponder the future, look at the opportunities, and smile within. There is no room for panic or sadness, other than I will miss her as a team member. I will seek and select the best person possible to fill her slot. I sit here and think of what's in the checkbook. There is about

$4,500 and bills mount to over $11,000, and I know God knows these bills are due. He will provide as He always has. I cannot panic over something I don't have. I must continue to do His work and the provision to survive and succeed will come from Him.

Your Child, Linda

10/26/95 ~ 5:20 p.m.

It amazes me how good God is all the time. Last pay period, I had to borrow $7,000 from the line of credit to make payroll. The checkbook is low $6,000. Bills high, $40,000, and today God delivered a check for $41,000+.

Mary Salim knows that what we do is God's work and it was Him who created FDSA. How can we fail? Would He let something of His fail? We know, NO! As I sit here and relax, I smile as I think of all that has happened this week. I applied for a $50,000 line of credit, awaiting results. I spoke with Judy Thomkins in Anaheim. We may be able to form a partnership. I am awaiting further dialogue.

I pray that I never lose sight of His vision.

10/31/95 ~ 4:30 p.m.

Yesterday we received the PAN Contract. Lord willing, we will receive clients through the Aerospace closure.

I spoke with Judee in Anaheim about a possible partnership. She will obtain contracts, we will teach. Good private dollars. Like past work with Compton, I will reply to the upcoming Request for Proposal (RFP).

I am grateful to God. We will be able to make payroll and pay a few bills this Friday. He continues to carry us. I ask for His guidance and I also seek His help in removing the blockade in Sacramento.

The LVN Program meets all of the state regulations but our consultant Marcia Peterson seems to find reasons to make changes. The changes do not affect the content or its quality. God help us.

11/11/95 ~ 1:17 p.m.

The Vocational Nurse Program is submitted. Again, we wait. The school was reinstated into Community Hospital of San Bernardino. I pray for a great enrollment.

Our cash is tight but God has an abundance. He paid the bills last week, and there is more due this coming Friday. I know He will provide.

Yesterday, Cherry and I discussed the possibility of opening a home for pregnant, unwed ladies and using state funds to support it. I tell you what two minds can do. Lord, this would be just a delightful opportunity to assist young ladies in continuing their growth in education, finances, and spiritually. If it is to be, You will guide us.

We continue to go forth with God's help. My mind and my heart are open to receive Your blessings.

11/14/95 ~ 10:40 p.m.

I just spoke with Sadiq (my brother who is incarcerated), and I feel wonderful. I am so proud of him and his growth. God is good. God paid our bills this week, thank You.

Several things are in the pot. Contracts, child care, and I'm seeking a bus. God, guide us. We are preparing for the Holidays.

Lord, thank You.

Linda L. Smith

11/17/95 ~ 8:50 a.m.

I feel joyful and prayerful. God allowed me to rise to see a new day. Did I mention I mentor a young lady at Sierra High School? I hope to be an encouraging and supportive individual in her/our contact.

Today, we have a graduation. It totally delights me to have individuals graduate. It is such an achievement for them. Lord, thank You.

You have placed several things before me. I pray for completion of all tasks. Four-D Success Academy was built on Your love for us.

I see so much. The opportunity for growth is so great. I must become more involved with my work. There are times I feel non-productive and inactive.

I am so thankful to God for the calls I get from Sadiq. He sounded great, peaceful, and happy. Lord, guide me in my role to aid him. Give me the strength, finances, love, patience, and whatever else I need to do what You have in store for me.

I love the Lord so much. I am His child. I error, but He forgives.

Well it is 8 a.m. and it's time to get started.

Thanks.

11/17/95 ~ 1:40 p.m.

The LVN agreement was signed by the Community Hospital of San Bernardino. YES, YES, YES! ☺

Thank You.

11/27/95 ~ 5:20 p.m.

I met with DON/DSD at Bixby Knolls today. Things look extremely positive. Four-D will have training on site starting January 8, 1996 in Long Beach. The LVN Program is coming along great.

God is good!

11/29/95 ~ 3:41 p.m.

Today, Charlie, Jeff, and Davon began the interviews for Dawn's replacement. I am sad to see her go, yet excited about our future.

I met the new DON at Saint B's. Her name is Phillis Woods. It was a great meeting. She will see to it that our agreement is processed and signed by the end of the year. Tomorrow, Cherry and I are going to Sacramento for closure of the LVN Program.

God is good.

12/8/95 ~ 5:25 p.m.

Today we had a wonderful spirit-filled Graduation. The student's participation was excellent with prayers, speeches, singing, and presentation. Ms. Rita Aries 3rd Ward Council Woman was present and spoke along with other guest speakers.

I am so blessed to have the opportunity to work at Four D Success. I am blessed to have such a wonderful and supportive staff. God is good, all the time.

The Vocational Nurse Program is moving right along. I truly am anticipating the start of the class. It will be a day of praise and celebration. I take time to pray. Sometimes I must STOP, get still, and breathe in His goodness and say, "Thank You, Lord!"

I am working on establishing in San Diego. I drove to El Centro and made two cold calls, obtained good info, then drove to San Diego for a Tuesday morning appointment. I desire to be on site at the Metro Division and establish a child care center.

As I look forward to tomorrow, I realize God is always good. All bills are paid. Students are employed or will be by the 15th (I insist).

The DSD class had 8-9 students. Growing is good.

I know my fathers are watching over me.

Daddy, I thank you so much for your teachings, prayers, and love. Thank you for your counseling and honest communications. God bless your spirit. You have provided me with an understanding of God's power like no other.

Your time with me was not in vain.

I love you.

Oh yes, we obtained signatures from San Bernardino Community Hospital for the LVN+CNA program. Saint B's says they will sign. Both facilities received a call from Sacramento. This is an excellent sign. January 30, 1996 is coming. The Sacramento trip and meeting Ann Shuma proved positive!

12/14/95 ~ 5:35 p.m.

Oh what a week!

I awakened yesterday morning about 5 a.m. with an intense need to go to Long Beach to obtain a City Business License. I have the urgency to do everything right for set up. I called Sacramento and left a message for Howard to notify him of changes. Then I called

LA and spoke with the Council Rep Greg. All is well. Things are going smoothly.

The LVN Program is moving along. After close to 2 years, it's coming together. The staff contacted the hospital to verify the facility agreement. What a positive sign. We have 30 students enrolled. God has truly blessed us. Today I was notified that I was being selected as someone who has made a difference in SB County.

This next entry reflects my humble beginnings up to December 17, 1995

12/17/95 ~ 3:57 p.m.

It's December 17th 1995 at 3:57 p.m. and I'm sitting in my bedroom looking out the window. I am going to record the beginning of Four-D Success Academy, or at least attempt to. There is so much that occurred in the last four/five years, that it would be just absolutely impossible to put everything into this recording, but I will give some highlights.

As a young child at age five, I lived at 1450 North Mt. Vernon, and I remember very clearly going through a magazine and seeing a picture of a lady in a white uniform who was a nurse, and I knew at that tender age I desired to be a nurse. I wanted to help others. It was just pure and simple to me. Why not be a nurse? In my senior year, I attended San Gorgonio High School, and many wonderful things happened to me in terms of personal growth and development. One of the good things that was most rewarding was that I enrolled into a nurse assistant training program, and in a year I learned what a nurse assistant was to do and why she was to do it. Upon completing that training program, I obtained work at Del Rosa Convalescent Hospital, which was the facility where I trained.

Linda L. Smith

After working one year there I transferred to San Bernardino Community Hospital and worked. After a year and a half, and after putting in two years at San Bernardino Valley College, I transferred to Chaffey College and Santo Antonio Community Hospital.

I was accepted into the RN Training Program at Chaffey College. I remember wearing a pair of red shoes, a blue skirt with a white blouse, gloves, and I had a red, white, and blue purse. I felt really proud of myself. I knew what I wanted to do. I had been raised with such a good character and character reference. I was so pleased to hear that I had been accepted into the nursing program and that there had been 111 or more on that list, meaning there were 110 people on that waiting list before I had even applied and I had been accepted over them.

At the completion of the training program, I did numerous things. I was a charge nurse. I worked for the Public Health Department as a Supervisor. I was an Admissions Coordinator for an Acute Hospital. I was a triage nurse at Kaiser for over six years.

While at the Health Department, I decided I wanted a bigger challenge and I took on the role of a director of nurses in a skilled facility. And after 18 months of living and breathing that facility, I realized that I could do what the Nurse Consultant was doing when she came into my facility. I could take all that I had learned in 18 months because I felt I had learned so much and I had consumed so much knowledge that I could provide the same, if not better, level of care and advice to my peers.

I eventually quit my position as Director of Quality Assurance and called everyone I knew and told them I was in business for myself as a private Nurse Consultant. Many people told me I would not make it and, to their surprise, I did receive the calls and I had a private job assisting in organizing a nursing department for $5,000 for my first contract. My second contract was preparing a hospital for state review for a fee of $15,000. While performing those duties, I received a call from a corporation asking me to come on board. I agreed to go after I completed my last assignment. I was given the challenge of being the Corporate Nurse Consultant for skilled facilities.

I was assigned 12 nursing facilities, five of which did not have a director of nurses. It took me a year and a half to stabilize my region. I trained over 22 RNs to become director of nurses before stabilizing the area. I developed my own director of nursing training manual and I reached out and began to provide nursing services as I had been taught.

While working for the corporation, I had requested to have a room where I could provide training services for nursing assistants. I felt that Nurse Assistants had very low self-esteem. They did not know what they were to do and why they were to do it. They did not have a very good base. After being told that there were other things the company wanted me to do, I began to really look within.

I wanted to train Nursing Assistants, and I began to pray and ask God to show me how. One of the nurses that I worked with was a staff developer who also taught with the Whittier ROP. I went and talked with the Administrator at the Whittier ROP just to find out what their process was, but to my surprise he introduced me to the supervisor who was also an instructor. She asked me to come and see a class, and I did. While I was there, she informed the students that I was a new instructor with ROP and that I would be taking over half the class. That was to my surprise. So, I in turn did not deny it. I simply asked the instructor if she would show me her lesson plans and her sign-in schedule. She had no lesson plans. Her sign-in schedule and her grading sheets were unorganized and not legible. I was totally appalled that the instructor did not have any organization to her process.

I was given a book and 10 students. I told those students that came with me that they could make a choice. If they came with me and stayed, it was with the understanding that I expected them to excel, and I expected them to be on time. I had noticed when the women arrived late at the other class, the instructor was not concerned about their arrival. They were late, they talked, it was totally disorganized, and I would not operate that way. They would have tests that I would develop. I would expect them to prepare for those tests and pass them, and if I found a student did not pass a test, that student would retake that test. That's what I was about. I was about teaching, they were about learning, and we were going to be about patient care. If they wanted to stay, fine. If not, they could return back to the chaos that they had just walked out of. All 10 chose to stay and all 10 graduated and did very well in their finals and continued on with their lives.

I began to ask God to show me how I could help others. You see, there was a period in my life when I had gone through a great deal of turmoil with my mother. That will be unexplained at this time, but the outcome of it was my understanding of the Word when it says, "Through pain, there's joy." I could stand and say, "Through God, all things are possible," and that if we just put our hand in His, He will bring us through all the trials and tribulations. And if we walk in the light, we will be OKAY.

As I began to pray, I asked that He take the very best of me for I know that He knows me better than I know myself. He knows my good, my bad, He knows my past, and He knows what lies in my future, and I am so grateful that He takes the very best of me and gives me a foundation where I could help others.

God began to work with me, and through me, and for me, and I began to meet individuals who began to help me formulate ideas about Four-D Success. I was in church and the Pastor asked, "How long have you not done what you wanted to do?" I had not done what I wanted to do. Six months later he asked, "Who has done what they have wanted to do?" and I had still not responded.

I said, "Lord I sure need help," and He began to work and I began to meet individuals.

I began to write a brochure and work with a young lady named Marry Anne. We developed a brochure, and when it was done, it had everything I initially wanted. It had the Home Health and the Acute Training Program. I still did not know what to do with this, and Mary Anne gave me a clipping out of the paper one day that talked about JTPA free training. I had asked God that whatever I did in this program, that I do it free for the clients who came to the school, but I really did not know what it was going to be. I simply wanted to work out of my garage, have one class in my garage, and be content.

As I prayed, and as He guided me, I wrote a proposal to JTPA and I asked the network at a meeting from the State. She said, "When I come to your office…" and I thought *My God, I don't have an office.* So I contacted a dear friend of mine and said, "Mike, I need an office. I need it on Foothill in Claremont, .50 cents a sq. ft. and free rent for the first four months."

Mike looked at me and said to me, "You talking prime location, prime city ... I don't know." He came to me a few weeks later with a prime location, prime city, and with free rent. A proposal was submitted and approved by JTPA, and in September 1992, I began to teach a class of two students.

Before I even get to that point, let me share with you the night of June 30, 1991. I was awakened from a deep sleep by God who told me to get up and write. I really looked at my clock and said, "Lord, it's 1:05 in the morning. I'll remember it today, and write it in the morning." God kept calling me, so believe me, I got up. I got a pad and went into the bathroom and I sat on the commode and said, "Okay, Lord, what do I write?"

I wrote <u>DESIRE</u> = desire to achieve. <u>DETERMINATION</u> = to follow up the process. <u>DRIVE</u> = the energy level needed to be consistent. <u>DELIEVERANCE</u> = reaching your goals for success. I said, "Okay, Lord, I got this, but I still have to have a motto. I have to be willing. Who is it that I want to help? Because I really don't know."

I began to think about who would be in most need, and I thought, what do I want to do with all this? I want to be this teacher, this example of the care, compassion, and kindness that is needed to be a nurse. I want to teach that they are to extend that high level of care and kindness to the patients that they serve. I wanted to be an alternative to help individuals who are in need and could look at a different way of life. I wanted to create an opportunity of learning. I wanted to create a new beginning in others.

I had gone through my own personal trial, and I have seen what God can do because He did it to me, and for me, and I have asked Him for a foundation where I can stand before others and say, "Through God, all things are possible." Once I wrote that, I drew a picture on this piece of paper of a cobble street, and on this street I put a lamp, and I thought about a scripture, "a lamp unto my feet, a light unto my path," and I thought, "Lord, this is as long as I walk on the path that is lit by You. I will never go wrong, and I shall never fear for what I do is in Your Name. So Four-D Success is Your school, and I am only an instrument that You will use and I thank You.

On August 2, 1992, I moved in and opened Four-D Success Academy in Claremont at 987 West Foothill, Suite D in Claremont. On September 17th, the Department of Health Service came to visit and after reviewing the program and the policy and procedure manual she informed me that it was one of the best programs she had ever seen written by an individual. She wished me much success and she handed me my papers to operate.

On approximately September 25th, I received and enrolled two students from San Bernardino County for my very first CNA training program. In November, I started an evening class. I had a schedule where I worked 8-2 in the morning teaching, and from 4-9 in the evening teaching and in between I wrote a program for the Acute Nurse Aide Training and the Home Health Aide Training Program. I got approvals for the Duarte site, San Bernardino site, and for Riverside. I worked like there was no tomorrow.

In February 1993 I hired Adenia Williams to come and work with Pam and I. Our work had only just begun. Today, Four-D Success Academy is located in Colton, California with a staff of 10, and we also have a site in Riverside, and we will be opening in Long Beach. We continue to seek proposals to provide free training to individuals who want to enter into health care. God has blessed us with the opportunity to start a Vocational Nurse program in January. I know through Him that this program will be one of the best in California. Not simply in its material, but in its delivery from staff.

I have been very blessed by God to have a staff who understands the philosophy of the school and that I believe through God, all things are possible. I believe that every man, boy, woman, and girl is a child of God. I believe that God has given us an opportunity to reach out and help someone else, making a difference in their lives. I believe that through my life, and through my example of my touching others, that He has given me this opportunity as He has given to staff, to make a difference in someone's life.

I am very grateful to have a staff that can pray and acknowledge God's presence in their lives. Through our example as a team, we exemplify what we write in our philosophy and our belief in God that mankind is here to provide service to another. As humans, we owe it to one another to help. God gave His Son to us all, and we are required to give a little bit of our time and love to a stranger.

I am very proud to be employed by Four-D Success and I am very pleased to have been chosen by God. For whatever reason, He gave me this task. Maybe He gave me this task simply because I asked that He take the very best of me, and allow me to stand before someone else and say, "Through God all things are possible." I am grateful for all that He has given me. I am grateful for everyone that He has put in my path because as I have grown, and as I have been molded, it has been the result of the individuals whose paths I have dared to cross.

The wonderful contacts I have made with God have been good for He has provided. God has continued to allow us to grow to a staff of 10 at this present time. With two sites, and one coming, and He still pays the bills.

There were times that the checkbook was extremely tight and my monthly operations run me $40,000-45,000 a month. There were times when I had less than $5,000 in the bank but the checks came in, the bills got paid as they always do, and as they always will. I know many people don't think I'm very orthodox in my management of Four-D, but I think that's good. See, I don't know that there are formulas that will tell me whether or not I'm making money. And maybe I don't care because I didn't go into this business to make money. I went into this business simply to say that God is real. I went into this business to teach individuals who wanted to be Nursing Assistants how to do it right. To create a theory-based training program that would elevate them above the norm.

I am not concerned about how much money we make. I know the business has to make money in order to survive. I know the business has to make money to pay its staff to operate, but I know what no one else needs to understand that my banker's name is truly God. And I worry like every other owner would worry, but when I get tired of it, I realize that I worried needlessly. Because if Four-D Success does not continue to function, I believe in my heart it's because God has something else for me to do. Right now, we are on a growing mode and He is putting individuals in my path that can guide me and who can help me, and money is not my concern, so I don't know all the formulas to making money. Again, that's not what I came here for. But I do know the formula to help. Thank You.

This ends my personal reflection on the day of December 17, 1995. I trust you are encouraged and inspired to reach beyond your grasp, and into the mighty hand of God according to the plans that He has for you.

12/19/95 ~ 4:40 p.m.

On 12/15/95, I flew Sadiq's sons and daughter Jamila to see him. The anticipation was high. His twin sons Anwar and Jaise just kept talking about their daddy. Going to their daddy's house, staying at their daddy's house. Jamila's silence reflected her deep thoughts and anticipations. The children had not seen their dad in two years.

When Sadiq laid eyes on his sons, tears came immediately to his eyes. A smile covered his face. He looked at me and all I could do was nod. Then he began to rapidly roam the room with his eyes looking for his daughter. Unable to spot her, for she was bent over, looking into a vending machine, he asked, "Where is Jamila?"

"There," I said, "at the machine." A moment of peace, joy, excitement, high emotions, seemed to move across his face. He realized his baby daughter was growing up. She was tall! When she stood up, turned, and saw her dad, she grabbed him with full force as he did with her. They embraced for a while, sharing tears of joy.

I sat, slept, and reflected on how grateful I was that God had given me this opportunity. He had given me the resources to do this. As the day came to an end, we began to say our goodbyes until the next day. It is indescribable to express what it was like watching him play with his kids and hearing the word "Daddy."

We returned on Saturday the 16th for another day of fun, love, kisses, and joy. He talked, laughed, touched, played, and ate with his kids. He played dodge ball, kick ball, and gave piggy-back rides. He shared his food and embraced all he could for the time they had. I sat, prayed, and patiently waited for our moment to say goodbye.

We never know what's in store for us. We pray that we are always prepared or at least willing to comply with God's direction.

Thank You, Lord for all. Thank You for Sadiq's joy!

12/19/95 ~ 5:05 p.m.

I recorded a little history of FDSA, typed it, and today Marie Chang printed it out. I spoke spontaneously from my heart for 30 minutes. When I was done, I cried.

So much has occurred in the past 4-6 years. So much joy, pain, and influence. But God has always been the same. He continues to provide, pay our bills. In fact, ALL of this month's bills are paid and we have a balance of $5,793.28. This does not include the $41,000 to come this month.

We had been waiting for a $14,000 check to come and it did today! BILLS PAID.

God guides us daily.

We are submitting to the Council for the VN Program. All is well. Greg Benton first noticed our lamp and scripture. He is a Christian and has a Masters in Theology Studies. He understands our mission and purpose. We showed the fact that we pray for our students' success. We are thankful to God to have the opportunity to do this work.

Lord, thank You.

153

12/21/95 ~ 4:25 p.m.

Today is a blessed day. We had a potluck of gumbo, rice, salad, peach cobbler, and ice cream. Oh what good eating and laughter there was.

I am truly so blessed to be in this environment. It truly is indescribable the joy these ladies bring. The only person missing was Cherry, and what a time she missed.

I spoke with Sadiq today. I am so happy he and I can share and console one another. He is fine, and God is good.

The New Year will be busier than ever. We are going to triple in our productivity. I know Mary Salim says, "Never put limits on what you ask God for. He may want to give more and we ask for less." We all are open to His plentiful blessings and a triple increase in clients and revenue will be great!

We ended the June 30, 1995 fiscal year with $571,150 for gross sales.

Our accrual was $632,960.

All I can do is smile. He knows my heart!

12/27/95 ~ 4:43 p.m.

On Sunday December 24, 1995, I was listed as 1 of 10 who has made a difference in the Inland Empire. What an opportunity my God has given me! The opportunity to give my time, attention, and love to help someone else. I am so grateful to do this work!

Today, I had a couple, Mac and Tamara, bring their 1990 Blue Chevy Blazer for viewing at my house. I have always asked God to allow me to give my girls anything they wanted and to allow me to have the ability to provide for them. Aisha is thrilled, so am I. Thank You, Lord. Her dad asked if we could give Aisha's old car to her sister for a reduced cost. God always blesses us. Give her the car! Thank You, Lord!

Changes are coming for us. The state process is changing. God will guide us! The New Year 1996 is going to be wonderful.

12/29/95 ~ 3:24 p.m.

Oh, what a blessed day. Today we shared three things that we feel blessed with. God has truly worked through each of us. It was so wonderful to hear each employee reflect on God's goodness and love. The peace and joy He has given them. I am so grateful for this opportunity. If He closed us today, I know I have done what I was supposed to do. I was to use the foundation He gave me to show His love with others, to introduce Him to others, and to pray with them. I am happy with Four-D Success Academy. It is my home away from home. It gives me peace, love, happiness, and joy. It fills my empty space and transforms my tears of pain and sorrow to joy. It is an area of my life where I know I have been obedient to God to do His work, to spread His love.

I know He will continue to care for all of us as He always has. I pray for our continued unity of love and support that we have for one another.

Today, I spoke with Sadiq. How happy he is. God has truly filled his life with good things.

I'm pleased with him. Four-D Success Academy, Inc.

Lord, I love You and all that You stand for...

155

1/6/95 ~ 10:45 a.m.

Oh what a New Year! Last week, Pam and I had a meeting with the Riverside Private Industry Council (PIC), Supervisors, Pat Ramos, Gerry Craig, Loren Sims, Penny, and another lady. We're discussing Support Services, its problems in meeting the client's needs, and how to correct them. Well, it's possible we will be responsible for the paperwork and the Riverside office will be responsible for the billing and payment.

While meeting, I began to inquire about the December 15th memo about training, time limits, and cost limits. Our LVN Program exceeded the $6,000 + 9 month limits.

Well, this week has been a minor emotional rollercoaster. I say minor because I kept asking God, "What do I do next?" I was told that there was a possibility students who had been referred could not come based on the move. That's 17 people, which is ½ our enrollment. Well, Dorothy Warren, an Individual Referral case manager got on the bandwagon for us. She helped solve the problem. She spoke in our favor. Pat Ramos met with Cherry Houston. We must discuss the outcome. At least 15 students are eligible to start 2/5/96.

I spoke with Consultant Marcia Peterson. I inquired how the VN Program was coming. She stated it was going to the board with a recommendation for approval. Lord, to hear those words! Thank You. We have much to do, but we will get it done.

I did the orientation for 3 new nurses at Bixby Knolls in Long Beach. We will start the CNA on 1/9/96 and the HHA Program on 1/8/96. What a blessing. I had prayed for PRIVATE funds and here they come.

One of the nurses, Mary Sugimato (RN), and I will talk about FDSA program going into other cities in that area.

I know God watches over us. I know we will make it. I know I just need to keep asking Him what I should do and continue to pray that He sends us what we need. I pray that those who come to us be of good character in spirit.

I sit in my office looking out of the window, and I smile with tears and amazement of how God has used me, and what He has given me. I know that Four-D Success Academy, Inc. does not exist because of me. I exist because of Four-D Success Academy, Inc.

Forever grateful, Linda

1/18/96 ~ 10:05

I feel so blue today. I feel the struggle to keep us alive. I know God is carrying us. Yet, I feel anxious when the account is so low. I must wait on funds and continue to pray that income comes before payroll is due. He has provided us with a line of credit and I am thankful.

I feel like externally I look okay, but internally I am dying from sadness. My marriage has no joy, laughter, or the sense of being 'in love'. I give so much to work that it has fulfilled much of the void I have felt at home. I guess the dream I had last night is so vivid in my mind.

For the first time, I told Ernell, without fear, how I felt. I told him that we don't do anything together that is fun. I asked him if he can think of the last time we went out together and had fun. The last time we talked and laughed together. His nonchalant responses pushed me to a point of no return and he still seems OKAY.

A dream of reality, I feel blue today!

1/25/96 ~ 10:10 p.m.

I have reflected over the past few days and evaluated my situation. I see that I have crossed an invisible line, which has placed me beyond a point of pain or sorrow. I see how I got here and wished to God those whom I was seeking attention and help would have been more receptive.

I am blessed today as always. Today the orientation was held for the VN Program. There were at least 20 individuals present. I don't know what the start number will be, but we are there.

Tomorrow, Cherry and I are going to San Diego to hear the approval of the program. Today, I spoke with Mr. Benton about the Long Beach site and the approval for the program by the 'council'. He understands our urgency and need.

Tomorrow is payday and God delivered a check for $441,000+. Thank You, Lord. Bills are paid. He continues to bless us. We continue to bless others. Michelle Daisy crossed my mind today. I truly miss her.

1/30/96 ~ 1:35 p.m.

I must stop a moment. Four-D Success Academy was approved for its Vocational Nurse Training Program by the Board of Vocational Nurses and Psychiatric Examiners on 1/25/96 in San Diego California. It's amazing how God has pulled this together, and yet in our finest hour of being approved, a representative from Summit requested we be denied because we are ½ a block from her facility. She felt we would interfere with her ability to obtain facility contracts.

God is good. We are still accepting students into the Program, which will start February 5, 1996.

I submitted a letter to the Institute of Black Parenting, requesting to provide CPR and 1st Aide to their members.

I am applying to ABHAS for Accreditation. We are definitely going to need it to be in the marketing of receiving students and teachers.

I know He watches over us! Thank You, Lord.

2/2/96 ~ 5:35 p.m.

God brought me to my knees. I spoke with Mr. Greg Benson from the Council. I stressed the need for his approval for the LVN Program. Class was starting on Monday 2/5. We discussed issues, and he gave his verbal approval for the program to start. I am so filled with joy and happiness for Four-D Success Academy.

We prayed and gave thanks to God!

I sit in my office, my desk completely covered with paper from this week's activities. It has been busy. There is much to do, much to accomplish. Stay focused and in God's light. Our path shall never go dim.

All I can do is smile when I see God's plan...all I can do is smile.

Lord Jesus, Thank You.

2/6/96

Yesterday, the LVN students arrived. The class consists of 19 students. We are so grateful to God for this wonderful opportunity. We ask that He continues to bless us.

Thank You, Lord. We prayed as a group. My heart is filled with joy.

Linda L. Smith

2/19/96 ~ 7:55 p.m.

What a blessed day. I met with Beth Foster, VP Nursing at Redlands Community Hospital. She recognized me from the Newspaper article, '10 who *made a difference!*' We discussed the Training site for the CNA and LVN Program. We will meet in March with Cherry and her department heads.

I visited a Skilled Nursing facility that is interested in our CNA work and Training at their facility. God meets all our needs.

Pam and I met last Friday. I tried to press upon her the need to grow as a Supervisor. She stated she didn't have the time to <u>read</u>!

I asked God to prepare FDSA, and me for any and all changes that come our way that may have an impact on the school's operations. I know He will care for all.

I am so grateful to God for Four-D. I am so pleased to help others.

He guides our path.

2/26/96 ~ 2:16 p.m.

I met with Advisory Member E. Carrillo to discuss non-profit "Friends of Four-D Success" pitfalls. I can't be listed as President for both organizations. The Non-Profit will not belong to me, and it's scary to not have control of the daily operations, an ideal I am going to bring about. It is so important that the direction of the non-profit stay focused. I just pray for guidance. We also discussed the bookkeeping services fees, contracts, etc. I am extremely pleased with bookkeeping services. Denise provides more than tracking dollar and cents. Her availability exceeds the 9-5 hours. We have established trust and a positive work relationship.

Dr. M. S. Khan and I discussed the pay for his services. He agreed to accept my offer to provide instruction to the LVN Students. God is good. We have an M.D. on staff. This morning, I spoke with Accrediting Bureau of Health Education Services (ABHES). We are submitting our application for accreditation. Goal: June.

Guide us, Lord.

3/1/96 ~ 5:15 p.m.

Oh what a blessed day this has been! First, I went to Community Hospital of San Bernardino to meet with Tony Jackson, the Director of Pharmacy. I received two 1995 PDR's. He and I briefly discussed the Pharmacy Tech Training Program. I wish to develop a program for the 1996-1997 year. I met with Alea at Public Enterprise Center. We talked and prayed. I left there feeling absolutely wonderful.

The graduation was so spiritual, positive, and emotionally moving for me. The students' growth was tremendous. I just give praise to God for what He has allowed Four-D Success to do. I sit here thinking about Pam Jackson and I smile. We have come a long way.

Heavenly Father, I thank You oh so much for ALL that You have allowed us to do. We ask and pray for Your continued guidance and blessing. Lord, what do I do next? Keep my heart and mind OPEN to Your presence and direction. Your Grateful Child, Linda

3/13/96 ~ 11:12 p.m.

Today has been a day in which I have felt a great deal of pressure. The work relationship between Marie and Pam is strained. There seems to be constant issues over the phone being answered and ineffective communications. I met with Pam, Margie, and Marie to, once and for all, dissolve this wasted energy. I pray they can work out their issues. I have given directions; now I wait for results.

Payroll taxes are due - $5,200. I need to transfer funds from the line of credit. JTPA takes forever to pay. I called today on students enrolled in the 2/5 class. They have yet to receive training order for billing. On the JTPA staff desk sits my invoice dated 1/17/96. Two months have passed and she has not forwarded paper for payment.

My desk was filled to all four corners. I felt smothered and lost. I have stayed this evening to accomplish something in the peace and quiet of these walls. Only the ticking of the clock was here.

Yesterday evening, I visited with Keith Lee at 7:00 p.m. on my way out for 2 hours. He gave me some good points for partnership with larger schools. I will look into this.

I spoke with Roselyn at SBCH. She may do marketing with us for CPR contracts with agencies/hospitals.

I felt as though I could flood with tears today. But I have too much to do. The tears subsided, the prayers went up, and I felt a little better. I pray and ask God to send me help, help to generate revenue for survival and growth.

There is so much I want to do with my limited skills and resources. I know He will provide me with what I need.

Lord, thank You. Your faithful child. Tired but not weary. Beat but not lost, for God is good – ALL THE TIME!

3/26/94 ~ 12:54 p.m.

Several days ago, I felt relieved. I had spoken with Sadiq who insisted I speak to our mother about another sibling and his possible drug habits. He was concerned of the danger of his sons being exposed to his brother's activity. I stressed to him that his brothers lived in his mother's house and I had NO control of her environment. I spoke with my mother and expressed to her that she had control and it was her choice to allow him to live there.

I freed myself of that old wound. I am not responsible for my brother's actions. I can't assume responsibility for his incarceration, and cost of an attorney.

Today, I met with Bruce Bennett, the Adm. at Community Care Conv. and Rehab Center of Riverside. I requested the use of his land to establish a playground for the Child Care Center Four-D is going to establish. He agreed to let us use the land in exchange for his staff having access to the center at a nominal fee.

God is good. I simply must follow His plan!

4/20/96 ~ 3:00 p.m.

Much has happened since my last entry. Cherry has attended two workshops on international trade. We are interested in working with other countries. She also has met with the District Manager for the California Conservator Corp. The Pomona office is interested in us doing their educational components: GED, Computer Training, First Aid and CPR.

I met with the District Manager in the San Bernardino County area. I am seeking a contract for CPR/First Aid and Job Placement Services.

Next week Denise and I go to New York for training. We wish to be prepared for Financial Aid Services.

The accreditation visit is this Friday for preview. All is progressing well.

Maria Chavez resigned. She gave verbal notice on 4/9/96 that she had started looking for a new job and she would be gone by May 1st. I requested her written resignation since I was leaving on the 2nd for business. I honored her request and relieved her of her duties on April 9th.

I knew all things happened for a reason in the right season.

God, guide me daily.

4/26/96 ~ 7:26 a.m.

What a busy two weeks. I attended the JTPA Conference in Monterey, California, for one week. I didn't learn much. Everyone is waiting on the State Budget before much will be known for the upcoming year.

Prior to leaving, I did meet a lady named Karen Jones. She informed me of a person interested in schools doing training for the Government. I also met Sandie Phelps, who has a program on Pharmacy Tech Training. She is sending the program to me. My goal is to have the program established by or in 1997. Last but not least, I met Art Lilly, the District Manager of California Conservation Corporation, San Bernardino. We attended Valley College together. FDSA is interested in doing CPR, First Aid, and Job Placement for the youth CCC services.

I met Tim McCullough, a park planner, and requested he assist in the playground design for child care.

I met with Tom Rivera (Cal State SB) and Elizabeth Barfield, Chair of the Nursing Dept. at Cal State San Bernardino; we're trying to reestablish relationship for a Bridge Program for the LVN Students.

We are preparing to submit the accreditation Program to ABHES. Oh yes, I spent one week in New York! U.S. Department of Ed Training for Title IV Program. Much to learn, but accomplishable.

I spent the weekend in Niagara Falls, Canada. I had a wonderful time. The Falls are indescribable.

I have ideas from the workshop and for Rex Hollingsworth (Dir. Falison)...
- ✓ Establish non-profit
- ✓ Establish Corp. leasing Co.
- ✓ Open Child Care "My Child's Place"
- ✓ Open registry, "Integrate Nurse Services"

Goals to be established by June 1, 1996.

5/2/96 ~ 2:20 p.m.

There are no problems – only solutions. As we progress with the LVN students, there are hurdles to go over.

I visited my Dad's gravesite today. With so much on my mind, I sit and think, "Daddy, there is so much to do." I read his headstone, "Let your heart not be troubled. Believe in God. Also believe in me. John 4:1"

I got my answer.

I must trust and remember that I am in God's grace and presence at all times. He shelters me, protects me, and guides me. Four-D is His.

5/13/96 ~ 7:35 a.m.

So today, I come in feeling blue. Yesterday was Mother's day and two of my dearest friends informed me that they and their husbands are splitting up. One has three teenage daughters, the other has two young sons. I reflect on my life. I am saddened.

Four-D Success Academy is keeping me (us) busy. I am working on a child care center, and next week we will be reviewed for Accreditation. The teamwork here has been tremendous. God, grant me the wisdom I need to be a good leader.

Love Your child, Linda

5/17/96 ~ 7:35 a.m.

Last evening, I cried. I felt like a broken vessel. I have been wounded by the conduct of the VN Students. They have been dishonest, stealing the final pharmacology test and passing it out, fighting verbally, being disrespectful to each other and to the faculty. I am totally dumbfounded by all of this. To top it all off, Dr. Houston dismissed one of the instructors for non-compliance. Ms. R. had been written up, counseled, and it was evident that she would be a detriment to the program if left in place.

I ask God to keep us sailing in these rough seas. I ask that He show me how to direct this body with the aid of the faculty. I ask that He guide all of the students in the direction that they should go. Lord, You know me, oh so much better than I know myself. You know my heart, my spirit, and my desires. I pray that I continue to rely on You and stay in Your grace. I know and believe that through You, all things are possible. I thank You for bringing me this far.

With Love and Gratitude, Linda

5/21/96 ~ 6:30 a.m.

It has been a spiritual war. The atmosphere in the LVN room is so negative, you can cut it with a knife. Changes have been made.

First, I prayed. I asked the staff to lift the group up and pray. Second, we relieved the instructor Ms. R of her position. She lacked accountability of her actions.

I spoke with the students last Friday about accountability. I asked God to show me how to deliver my message and He did! On Monday 5/20, I went into their room with a prayerful heart. I spoke of love for them, my desire to see them achieve, the need for them to have a desire to learn and grow, and a need for a change of heart. They had to change their heart in order for their mind to accept the knowledge they needed. A closed heart affects our thought process.

Today, we are going through the accreditation process for Accrediting Bureau of Health Education. I know God has prepared us. We will be successful.

Lord, I thank You for being the wings on which I fly and the rock of my foundation. Your Child, Linda

5/21/96 ~ 7:25 p.m.

We made it through round one of the accreditation. Chris Easton and Ann Gibson were here. They were supportive, informative, and very encouraging. The outcome:

Two excellent areas over and above the norm:
- ✓ Organization of student files
- ✓ Maintenance of facility

Five standards to meet:
- ✓ Catalog
- ✓ CNA Program
- ✓ Storage of records

Linda L. Smith

I am pleased. The staff is to be commended for their high-quality performance. We will respond and be ready by May 30th.

Lord, thank You. I am tired, but happy.

6/11/96

Well, we have been busy. We have responded to the accreditation. The report will be marked off tomorrow.

The staff and I went on a cruise on the Royal Caribbean Viking Serenade from 6/7-6/10 and had a great time.

A student came into my office this morning to resign from the program. She voiced complaints I had never been informed of. She reported being pinched and slapped by an instructor.

The instructor admits to pinching the student on the arm when she accepted medication from another nurse to administer. She denies slapping the student. She will not do it again. The instructor was informed of legal issues and instructed not to touch a student.

Jesus, there are high walls ahead, raise us up and over. Strengthen me. Help me focus on all of my assignments.

6/17/96

Zack overdosed on Saturday morning. His behavior of violence is very unsafe in my mother's home. He refused to take his medication. When she approached him about it, he put a hole through a door. She removed the twins from the house and called the police. He was taken to Ward B. Because of his excessive drowsiness, he was taken to the

168

hospital for assessment. It was determined he had taken an overdose of Elavil.

While checking the door to the first bedroom, I noticed there was patchwork on the second door. Mother informed me he had put two holes in that door the previous week. How much will she take before enough is enough?

Donnie has been put out again. He's working, eating up everything, not paying for anything, and lying. He refused to return the house key until he receives his food stamps from her. How much more will she take?

I feel so helpless. How can I help without the pain of being emotionally drained? Do they even want my help?

I miss my dad! Lord, show me the way!

6/18/96 ~ 3:40 p.m.

We received a call from Cherry this morning from Washington D.C. She met with Joseph Mutaboba, PhD of Foreign Affairs for the Rwanda Embassy. She presented the Rwanda Education Project. He is very interested in Four-D Success providing education to his councilmen/women for Nursing Education, CNA/HHA/LVN and instructors.

I will be meeting with him when I go to Washington in July. I know we can assist them in some way.

I kneeled and prayed, giving thanks to God for this opportunity and blessing. I share my joy with the staff. The possibilities are awesome! We are making a difference in someone's life!

Thank You, Lord.

6/24/96 ~ 12:07 p.m.

God I feel good today. I feel like I am on TOP of the world. E. Hunt (LVN Student) came to me and shared how she studied this past weekend. She focused and found there was much to learn. She stated she was hungry to learn more. She studied until 4:00 a.m. She realized that she could no longer make excuses for not being successful.

I had her share her experience with her peers. I wanted them to hear someone who had a 'breakthrough' and found the value in application.

If I can help one to understand what I see, I will be blessed by God. I asked them to think of the worst scenario if they did not succeed here and to think of the best scenario if they succeeded. For E. Hunt, there will be no more welfare. We will all continue to achieve our best.

Lord, thank You for Your revelation to E. Hunt. I pray the others will open their eyes and heart to You and learning.

7/8/96 ~ 9:52

Well, I am back after a week in Washington D.C. and two days in Houston. I never had the opportunity to meet with the Ambassador. I sat in my room for two days waiting to be scheduled for an appointment. I knew if I didn't see him by Wednesday, then there would be no meeting on the 4th or 5th. I did fax him a note expressing my desires to meet him and introduce myself.

I attended my cousin's funeral, Calvin C. Johnson. Age 45. Died of a heart attack. Life is so uncertain.

I don't know where I am going to be in my personal life. I arrived home feeling indifferent after being in Washington D.C. Spending time alone, enjoying the sights and entertainment alone. I began to become relieved of my fear. The fear of Ernell's response if I said no – no to all the loneliness I feel in his presence, no to being afraid, no more.

Today, I have no fear of saying no.

We are scheduled to have class next week. Only two students have been referred from Riverside. I spoke with Kathy of Riverside and explained our situation. I discussed the need for students. The struggle never ends.

Denise called last night. We discussed the school's finances. The Corp revenue was $788,467.00 for 1995-1996. No money in the bank.

ABHES denied our application for accreditation. We need to comply and reapply by October 31, 1996 for the December review.

There are times I feel like a shell — hollow.

Whatever is happening is beyond me. God, grant me peace again. Grant Four-D Success Academy success.

Weary, challenged, reaching out to God.

7/20/96 ~ 1:55 p.m.

I come here on Saturday to pray and work. I need to sit still and talk with God. My troubles are His. Therefore, I seek answers to why I worry. I know He has not brought me this far to leave us here. Our mission is to praise Him and say His name, to introduce others to His goodness by our actions and deeds.

I know the personal turmoil in my life is affecting my concentration at work. My sadness sometimes overpowers me and my loneliness stumps me. I know that God is present. Sometimes I am not.

Although I am uncertain of our future here, I know God knows it. His plan will be revealed. I asked that He allow those who control the referral process of students to us to allow them to come expediently.

My father also reminds me that God didn't bring me this far to leave me. I wipe a tear from my eyes. I know he cared so much for me. I am grateful for his love and faith in God. I am so thankful that he took the time to share his love for God with me. He trusted in God. Knowing God only gave him what he could bear. He knew that God carried him. I must always remember that God carries me. He guides me. I must sit still and pray and ask the Lord: What do I do now? How do I achieve my goals? How do I improve operations? What am I doing wrong?

I sit here, looking out the window, asking Him to speak to me.

Thank You, Jesus.

7/26/96 ~ 5:56 p.m.

I met with the Deputy Director of Riverside JTPA, to discuss Four-D Success Academy's role with Riverside JTPA. She assured me that we are well-received by the office. We will have students for training.

I met with Keith Lee July 25th to discuss the drop in enrollment from 50+ students to 18 students. He indicated that all SDA received fewer funds for training. He will look into the reason for the drop. Today, Cherry and I attended a meeting with Access International. We are seeking avenues to do training to Africa.

God will guide us. I feel much better today after singing and praying. I know God will guide us. The future is BRIGHT. Our team is solid. I sing *Lead Me* and *Amazing Grace*. I praise Him and thank Him for all that He has done through me.

Lord, thank You for this day.

7/30/96 ~ 3:07 p.m.

This has truly been a trying week for me. I have been very concerned about the finances of the school. The referrals are extremely low. Private enrollment is low. Bills continue to be high.

My health has been affected due to worry. I have been on my menses for 2 ½ weeks. This has never occurred before. I sit and cry over all that I want to do. Those I want to help, staff I desire to keep, the programs to develop. I pray to God. I know He knows my heart, my needs, the school's needs, and the students' needs. I know He has brought us this far. He will not bring us this far to leave us without the means to continue.

I pray and sing my way out. I have an old gospel songbook. Thumbing through it, I came across *What a Friend*. I began to sing that song followed by *Lead Me*. Followed by *Amazing Grace*. I sang, I cried, and prayed until I began to feel His presence in me and healing taking place. Faith is so valuable and unexplainable. <u>My faith can weather the storm.</u>

Several students in the LVN Program were counseled today and put on probation. At times, one must be firm in the policy of the school. Students must be held accountable for learning.

Keep me focused, keep us all inspired, and keep our doors open. Heal my body, Lord. Ease my mind. Take us over the troubled waters.

Linda L. Smith

Your Child, Linda

8/9/96 ~ 9:41 a.m.

God has blessed Four-D with the financial means to pay salaries and some bills. I had to transfer $16,500 from the line of credit. I now owe $5,500+7,500+16,500= 29,500 to Bank of America. My limit is $35,000. I still have $50,000 with Wells Fargo. I know God will submit what we need. I pray for changes at the JTPA's so we can continue our role. I ask that God keep us in prayer and focused. I must seek accounts of payment that are due. We are climbing up a hill; we are coming out of the valley. I may need to look at a four-day workweek. I sit and ponder so many things. My personal life is crumbling at home. I feel frustrated and empty. I sing myself out of the hole.

God is good, all the time.

8/14/96 ~ 4:05

I am thankful for another day. We are in a financial crisis. All bills are paid. We have $760.00 in the account. There are some bills on hold. We are awaiting funds due to us from JTPA. I am trying every angle possible. I attended a Vendor's meeting in Compton. I have been approved for three years. This may be the year for us. I placed a call to Long Beach Memorial to request an appointment to meet with the DON. We are seeking a facility for training LVN and CNA. There is a new Administrator coming to Bixby Knolls Tower. I must meet her or him to establish continued relationship with the facility.

God will bless us. I have asked the staff to assist in maintaining our operations. I will assess where we are and pray for guidance.

174

8/21/96 ~ 7:40 p.m.

Lord I am grateful for another day. We will make payroll and bills. I assessed the accounts payable, and I am holding some so I don't have to go to the credit line! I met with Charlie Raymond Crawford and Ulric Jones to discuss financial issues at Four-D. I received their advice and I am grateful for their support. The team is doing well and producing 100%.

The DON seemed to want us out of Bixby Knolls Towers but I am addressing this issue with Mr. Niroff Intern Adm. I'll know his decision in a couple of days.

I pray for so many things. I lack total focus and attention. Seem to have multiple interruptions throughout the day and I feel I must address as much as I possibly can. I know I will complete my assignments.

Our future is bright and Four-D and staff will continue to provide its services to the community. I sit here and think of my father and his faith.

God is good, all the time. He put the roof over my head, clothes on my back, and food in my stomach. I have a little change in my pocket. What more do I need? GOD supports it ALL. ☺

8/22/96 ~ 3:05

I visited Alia at the PEC in SB. Shared God's goodness. She states one day I will be a billionaire. I smile and think to myself, "I just want to pay bills." I received a call from Bill Niroff, Adm at Bixby Knolls Towers. He has approved our stay at the facility. Thank you, Jesus!

Pam Jackson off for surgery. We prayed, Mary, Shirley, Cassandra, Margie and I. We know she will be okay. I will visit her tomorrow.

We are busy with our programs. We continue to move ahead.

My focus does not seem as keen. I've not slept well this past week. Loads of things are on my mind, I just keep saying September 12th will be two years since Daddy's death. I miss him so. We talk in prayer and spirit. When I am weak, I know he is saying, "God's taking care of you. Girl, you are going to be alright." I feel comfort.

We have three contracts to complete in the next 2 ½ weeks. Submit Accreditation paperwork. I need to focus on the Pharmacy Tech Program. Payroll made, I am happy!

Thanks.

8/29/96 ~ 5:00 p.m.

I had to scale down the staff. I placed Lanell on call as of 8/19/96, and yesterday I had to inform Shirley I could no longer keep her on staff. I tried to be strong. I heard a young man named John Hope speak at the African Chamber of Commerce and he said business is business, and you cannot run it on emotions. Emotions don't pay bills.

He was talking to EMOTIONAL LINDA.

The Medical Society approved my request to scale our rent to half for two months. Bixby Knoll's Administrator approval allows us to stay there.

I received a phone call that we have received 5 students for the 9/16 class. Robert Rochelle, my wonderful supporter in working on sending us more students. God has blessed FDSA with wonderful supporters. The Valley that we are in, I know God will bring us out.

9/6/96 ~ 6:25

Today, Mr. Sorsenson reduced my Riverside rent to $1,000 for four months without additional cost for November-December. Starting in January 1997, rent will be $2,200.

I attended a meeting with Ms. Rita Aries Council woman – doing business with the city of SB. She is supportive of Four-D Programs.

I feel better today, even though I think A. Rodgers has been over charging me on advertisement. I have an appointment with him tomorrow at 10:00.

We have individuals lined up for interviews for bookkeeping positions on Friday.

I am very grateful to God for all things.

9/16/96 ~ 5:39 p.m.

The bookkeeper I hired last Tuesday, called on Friday at 4:00 p.m. to say she was not reporting in on Monday. She has accepted another job. I didn't feel disappointed. Things happen for good reasons. I interviewed two ladies today. I felt most comfortable with Ms. Moon and she had the most experience. I will offer her the job to start Wednesday. We started the CNA Class with 11 students today. God sent us $7,000 today, I am working on the Non-Profit, LA County contract, Long Beach site, marketing, new bookkeeper, and monitoring staff. The staff has been superb working with me.

At times I feel overwhelmed and then I listen to the message from Church about "faith." Last Sunday, Pastor Crawford spoke about us having faith when we are at the trunk of the tree but we lose faith when we need it most, when we are out on the branches! That is when we must be rooted in faith. I have been on the branches. God is with me! He has not brought us this far to leave us. He cleans the path, which we follow. Sometimes I think of what I do and why I do it and I feel God's presence all around me and I cry. I know He carries me through the longest valleys. Four-D will reach its peak. I am so grateful for Robert Rochelle's support and prayers along with all others. His faith in God and belief in what we do continues to fuel his desire to help us succeed.

One day, I will learn that to worry has no value "for it does not change a thing." Action brings about changes. I must place my ad. I come to find out that Alex Rodgers has not been paying our bills on time. He could affect my credit with companies! I am truly disappointed in him. I will take over and run all ads from the Corporate Office.

I've asked Enid Hamilton to develop an In-Home Training Program for laypersons on how to take care of loved ones from the hospital. Kathy will develop an IV Training Program, and I met with Tony Jackson Pharmacist at SB Com Hospital about a Pharmacy Technician Program. We have things in the fire, with good opportunities ahead.

Lord, I thank You for so much my present state of mind, my positive spirit, my love of life and others. For the staff and Four-D Success.

Keep us together, let us all work for the betterment of others.

Your Child, Linda

September 12, 1994 Daddy died. It's been two years. Yesterday, I ran two stop signs while he was on my mind. He would have been 73 on 9/20/96. Daddy, I love you.

9/22/96 ~ 6 p.m.

Yesterday, I visited Sadiq. Aisha, Tahira, Anwar, Jaise, Eula Russ (mama), Walter Jr., Adelaja, Nirobi, Jamila, Takara went also. It was a 4-hour trip. We left my house at 5:30 a.m. and I arrived at 9:30 a.m. We visited from 10:00 - 3:00 p.m. It was a joy to see him with his kids. He looked great, in good shape, clean as usual.

At Church today, young men joined. I cried thinking of my 3 brothers who are incarcerated.

The new bookkeeper started last week. I am excited about the future.

The students are coming in. We started Monday's class with 11 students. We seek a full house from God!

Our blessing was to make payroll this week. God is good.

The Non-Profit final papers are complete and ready for mailing. "Friends of Four-D Success Academy."

Lord, thank You for all we have.

10/3/96 ~ 5:20 p.m.

Our beloved Rwandese students arrived on September 23, 1996, Innocent and Claire. Innocent is 28. He will attend Cal Poly University. Claire's 14, and she will attend the International High School at Cal Poly. Cherry's daughter, Catherine, and Claire share a birthday.

We had a welcome gathering at Don's house on September 28th. That was my first time meeting them. What a joy to be blessed to be a part of all this.

I met the new Administrator, Buck Perkins, at Bixby Knolls on October 1st, I could tell by his comments and questions he had been misled by the DON. He was told we would provide FREE Training to his nursing staff. It's obvious that he has not been given the truth. After our discussion, he indicated that the schedule would be worked out.

I stayed at the office until 12 midnight. I was drowning in paperwork and behind on projects, and the long hours proved effective.

I will be contacting the school Administrator at Compton Community College. I wish to establish an LVN Program there.

After my meeting with Mr. Perkins, I walked out feeling I should look for another place. I prayed, "God, show me where to go. Guide me." I got in my car in Long Beach and drove to Compton, zigzagging up and down streets. Somehow I ended in Lynwood, driving around blocks and blocks. The next thing I knew, I was in front of a sign that said Compton College. I turned right and I was immediately on the College grounds. Looking at the College, I said, "Lord, is this where You want me to be?" I then went to the Compton JTPA Office. I asked Reggie Allen if he had to open a school where would he do it. He circled around King Drew hospital.

I am attempting to schedule an appointment with the school Adm. God is good all the time! We need to push our enrollment for Riverside. It is still extremely slow but it will pick up.

Lord, thank You for my strength and courage. Keep me encouraged, focused, and productive. Thank You for the team that works with me.

10/15/96 ~ 8 p.m.

The last page in this book, but not the last entry of my voyage with Four-D Success Academy.

I established 'Friends of Four-D Success Academy,' and I am Pres/Sect, Cherry is V.P./Treasurer.

Cherry and I went to Detroit Michigan for the Africa World Expo. Great contacts. We met with President/Vice President of Comcast, Arthur Johnson. Great referrals: Alice Dear of the International Bank and Gary Lobster, Mayor of Saginaw, Michigan about possible Delegations to Nigeria 3/97!

Classes picking up ½ filled! More to come.

Spoke with Jane Singleton to assist with grant writing, and it's a go! First meeting tomorrow with Cherry and I. HHA program off to Sacramento

We will be holding classes at the Radisson thru November. Things will pick up. Thank You, Jesus...

10/24/96 ~ 8:36 p.m.

Last night, I felt totally emotionally overwhelmed. The financial burden is more than I want to hear. I cry out to my Jesus for help. He sees and knows where I am, He feels my pain, He knows my worry, I know He guides me, I know He is there. I know my faith in Him keeps me going. I ask Him to help me, help Four-D as I accepted my assignment. I have tried to fulfill my duties.

I feel full when we have graduations. I know we will always strive to help others.

Today, Four-D and I were interviewed by reporters with the Daily Press, Imadie Tate. What was to be a short meeting turned into a 3-hour interview. I can't wait for the print.

God, keep us. Open the doors that are shut. Send the finances to pay all bills and salaries.

My Love to You.

10/28/96 ~ 5:50 p.m.

This has been a blessed weekend. I spoke with Gregory Young. He is known for putting on excellent functions with Class! I requested his assistance in helping the Rwanda Education Project/Friends raise funds. He agreed to help. The revenue from his February 8, 1997 Birthday Party will be donated to us.

I called Irene Luna DAS in Sacramento regarding another school in Riverside. They are not approved to teach the Home Health Aide Program. I meet with Pat Ramos Riv. Super tomorrow. We received our "Sellers Permit." This will help us generate revenue through the school.

God is granting us favor. We ask to use it well.

Oh yes, Innocent went to Church with Aisha and I. Afterwards we went to dinner at Coco's. We had a good time. He is seeking a family to 'adopt' him. All members have agreed! I am happy.

10/30/96 ~ 10:45 p.m.

I have been on a writing campaign to stay alive. There is a school in Riverside teaching a CNA/HHA Program where the instructors are not approved to teach the HHA Program. I have written letters to Irene Luna, Keith Lee, Ernest Dowdy, Gilbert Lopez and M. Martinez in protest to the Employment Development Department (EDD) Board.

I have a meeting with Pat Ramos at 3:00 p.m. 10/31/96. I ask God for a listening ear from someone in that group.

"Guide us," we prayed as a group yesterday. What a wonderful feeling to know you are not alone. I met with Ruth Martinez and Michelle, Pomona City Assistant Administrator, seeking to establish a relationship to open a school. It's late and I am tired. I have a busy day tomorrow. Night, Lord.

11/4/96 ~ 4:45 p.m.

I don't see a way out of nowhere. After many cancelations with the Riverside JTPA management, I wrote a letter to the JTPA Directors, Ms. Luna RN Sup with DHS, voicing my concerns regarding the unlicensed school's operations. Well Lord, I surely don't know the outcome. No one is talking with me. Appointment cancelled today with Riverside. I am energized as I speak with Bill Young, LA County Special Projects. Maybe something positive will happen.

I have good ideals as well as the staff. We must have a breakthrough, Lord. Show us our path. Calm my internal spirit. I feel it rising with stress with finances. I can only continue to do this work.

Lord, help us please.

11/9/96 ~ 7:46

Yesterday, Cherry and I met with Dr. Culin. We discussed Four-D projects and Rwanda Education efforts. He inquired, toured the school, assessed, and then offered to aid us. He may see if a donation can be made to support the school from the proceeds of a fight he may promote. Lord, would that help with the rent!

Wells Fargo Bank increased the line to $15,000 more. After next week, it may go up $15,000-$20,000 thousand more.

The Lord will keep us here. Four-D Success Academy, Inc., is the only African-American approved Vocational Nursing School in California, and probably the U.S.

Cherry and I have great desires, and I know God will enable us to do more than 'hold on.' We (the entire team) will reach out and effectively make a difference in someone's life.

I presented a proposal to Regency Skilled Hospital to do ALL training through our LA County Contract. I shall know soon if they accept the offer.

11/21/96 ~ 9:50 a.m.

The Riverside JTPA Management has not responded to my calls or letters. I met with city officials. I spoke with Ms. Young Bureau for Private Post Secondary Vocational Education (BPPVE) and Irene Luna. Thus far, it appears no one is interested in the unlicensed school.

We have received few students, but God has kept us open and going.

I met with Ruth Martinez and Michelle Chan with the City of Pomona. They are assisting in our efforts for a location in Pomona.

I met Mr. Stanford Newton in Pomona. He is aiding our effort to obtain a site in Pomona.

LA County JTPA will place us on the Vendor list (3 months). I've been asked to write another proposal in order to do our own intake assessment etc. Lord, when does the confusion and uncertainty end?

11/29/96 ~ 4:35 p.m.

God has no limitation. Today, Cherry and I met Muhammad Ali, the greatest boxer of all time! It was at Borders Book and Music store in Santa Monica.

On Tuesday, November 26th, she and I attended the African Chamber of Commerce Meeting in Riverside, where the speaker talked about being persistent. On Tuesday evening, I heard a news flash of Ali and his wife's interest in Rwanda. I immediately called Cherry, excited about the news. On Wednesday she called across the U.S. and back trying to locate Ali. Then she called all the speakers we heard on Tuesday. Someone told her Muhammad Ali would be at the Borders Book store today. We couldn't wait to go.

We spoke with his assistant Howard Bingham and left the Rwanda Education Project with him. He assured us we would hear from him.

Our pictures were taken by Louis Villa. He had to stay with us until they were developed at the 1-hour photo at Woolworth's. We went back to Borders in time to say goodbye. We know we are at a breakthrough. We know that God is guiding us. The door is open, and we will walk through.

Jesus, thank You for guiding us.

Your Child, Linda

The song in my heart is *Lead me, Guide me.*

11/30/96 ~ 9:40 a.m.

Today, Cherry and I are totally elated about Muhammad Ali. I said, "In three years, we will have a 'RN Program.'" Cherry doesn't think we will ever have a RN Program. God will send us what we need!

12/3/96 ~ 12:45 a.m.

I am sitting in my den thinking, "What do I need to do to address the Academy's financial crisis?" I think every crisis is an opportunity to become creative and strengthened beyond boundaries, and take on challenges.

I will write out goals:

What do we need to earn each month? $40,000.

What will that equal in 12 months? $480,000

How do we get there? ... Here's the PLAN!

Schedule DSD (Director of Staff Development) class (6xmonth) various times; weekends and days (4xweek), evening (5 hours) 6 days;

Schedule IV Therapy 4 x months;

Provide classes in various parts of California.

Goal: DSD= $27,000; IV $10,000 with hire; clerk @ $8 hour; RN @ $20. Estimated cost for staff, travel, room, etc. $7,560-$8,000 (Tops) Profit $30,000.

Must implement starting in January '97.

Meet with Kathy and Enid.

Thank You, Lord for guidance.

12/3/96 ~ 1:42 a.m.

Awake and still in bed. It is revealed, "Out of every crisis, there is a benefit." This phase repeats continually in my mind. What is the benefit of a crisis?

1) Critical thinking develops as one seeks a positive outcome.
2) Goals established
3) Plans developed
4) Strategy implemented

One can dwell in the crisis until consumed or act to eliminate the crisis. I chose to "ACT."

12/10/96 ~ 7:15 a.m.

On Saturday December 7th, while going through the mail after returning home from the mountains with Ernell, I was filled with joy. I received a letter of congratulations from Supervisor Eaves for my work with Four-D and for being elected 1st Vice President of the National Council of Negro Women.

I shared the letter with Ernell. He had no response, no congratulations. He only asked, "Who is he?"

Life can be so empty at times.

I also received a copy of the letter Congressman Brown wrote to the Acting Adm. for the Department of Labor regarding the action (or lack of actions) by the Riverside JTPA Management.

God continues to bless us at the school. He keeps the door open.

The Riverside site is in serious trouble, but I truly have turned it over to God. If I must close it, then He will open another.

This Saturday, we are having our first capping/pinning ceremony for the Licensed Vocational Nurse students. God has brought us a long way. I was driving and singing *Lead Me* on my way to work. God is my guide, my strength, my comforter, my Father on earth and Heaven.

Your Child, Linda

12/10/96 ~ 10:50 a.m.

I received a call from Mr. Ferguson; we will be approved as a Charitable Non-profit Organization: Friends of Four-D Success Academy. I am delighted!

12/10/96 ~ 6: 55 p.m.

Met with Neil, manager at Riverside site. We discussed the need to reduce rent until further assessment of enrollees. We agreed to $250 a month for Jan., Feb., and March 1997.

Thank You, Lord.

Looking Back ...

- There are times when I have to take a moment to consider what He, the Lord, has already done! His faithfulness to FDSA and me is immeasurable. So during those moments of uncertainty, there are people within my immediate circle that can pray me through, and give me hope, and remind me of His love for me.

- No matter how large the vision gets, I must remember that I can do all things through Christ who gives me the strength to do what He has placed in my heart to do. And with that strength comes wisdom and a knowing that I can do this!

- Even in spirit, Daddy is always with me. He taught me by example how to pray and look to God. To him, I am forever grateful.

- This was my season to mourn and cry...no one is exempt.

- There are times when I may feel alone in my endeavors be they business or otherwise. Either way, I must always remind myself to stay focused. God is in control!

- Community presence is very important for many reasons, and recognition from the community is an honor and privilege when your works are being recognized.

- Excellence is not a question – it's a lifestyle in action. I keep myself ahead by setting my own boundaries. If the due date is the 10th, I'll change to it the 5th. That allows me time to review and make any necessary corrections if needed.

- His wonders never cease to amaze me. All I can say is *Divine Endorsement* is the best kind!

- I must always be honest with God, others, and myself. No one knows what I am fully capable of other than God and me. And there are times I know I can do more. I can do more because I have been entrusted with more… *To whom much is given, much is required!*

- Only God has the last word, and His word is always *yes* when I'm told *no*. Doors that close, close only for a moment!

- An effective leader can cast a vision that others can clearly follow. Team effort is a must to run a business efficiently and successfully. I have learned the importance of surrounding myself around a good team of people.

- Personal assessments are good. Every so often it's a good thing to stop and consider how far you have come. My heart flutters, and the tears flow when I think of the faithfulness of God in my life. What a mighty, mighty God I serve!

- Write the vision and make it plain! I learned how to do that early, and because of my dedication to the vision God has given me, it's been easy to share with others in both verbal and written form … AKA, proposals!

- I am an extension of God's love and grace to others: I extend His hands to comfort, I extend His words to speak kindness and wisdom, I extend His ears to listen with an attentive heart, and I extend His eyes to see the potential in others just as God does.

- To every situation, there is a solution!

- I have become accustomed to encouraging myself in the Lord. I sing songs of faith to restore my vision and hope in Him when whenever I feel the need to.

- Inspiration to press forward when things become a challenge can come from anywhere and anyone. It takes humility to see, hear, and receive the insight as it comes to you. During these fleeting moments of grace, I liken them to a gentle kiss from God, letting me know He's right there by my side.

- Always keep it moving! Turnover in staff is inevitable. Certainly you don't want to see productive people go, yet you must wish them well and immediately consider the best move for the business. Trust in your ability to recreate the flow and genius of solid team building to come shining through.

- A crisis will bring out the best in you, and the business. It is during those times that you allow your intuition, your creativity, and expertise as the leader to regenerate a spark of passion that will open up new endeavors and opportunities.

- When it's all said and done, if no one sings your praises, if no one pats you on the back for a job well done — it's okay. If they are singing your praises, and those closest to you seem to have a nonchalant attitude about your successes — again, it's okay. It's okay because using Jesus as our prime example; He too seemingly was not celebrated or received by His own people. Shake off the dust and keep your focus on the bigger picture before you — it's OKAY.

I totally depend on the childhood lessons of faith and love that my dear father taught me. And from his example to me, I purpose to be an example to those I come in contact with. Being that he was such a positive and prominent figure in my life, it took me some time to adapt to his physical absence. I'm thankful that I am able to feel him with me in spirit. The very thought of him brings a smile to my heart and a lift to my countenance. Walter Russ, Sr. will always play a significant role in the development of my character that is still maturing. I know that he would be exceedingly proud of my works, and for as long as I am able, I will strive to be the very best that I can be in God. For it is in Him that I live, move, and have my being.

Business by Faith

Journal 3

Begins: December 16, 1996 ~ 6:37p.m.

12/16/96 ~ 6:37 p.m.

Praise God! What an exciting weekend. On Sunday I, along with Aisha, Ernell and Innocent, attended Loveland Church. What a blessing. Afterward, Innocent and I went to Loma Linda to meet with Cherry, Catherine, and Claire, then we went over to Emmanuel Rudatsikira's house. He invited us over to meet his family and to share a meal.

My God, what have You blessed us with? To be a part of the gathering was awesome. To witness Innocent converse in his natural tongue with a fellow countryman was like being members of a family — a world apart together.

Claire had the opportunity to speak with Happy and Jean, Emmanuel's friend (Happy) and wife. She was blessed after a fulfilling meal and lovely conversation. Emmanuel took us to meet his parents. Lord, help me, the embrace sent me home with joy and peace.

His father, Minister Rudatsikira, is now retired. He retired in 1994. The missus embraced me and I held on. I laid my head against her shoulder and felt her loving arms encircle me. She held me like a child she loved. I received her love openly and she placed a kiss upon my cheek.

Minister Rudatsikira asked how all this came about. Cherry began her story and Emmanuel translated for his family. Although the minister speaks English, Kylawanda translation was lost. He and his wife thanked us for our efforts. He then asked Innocent to speak to him in his natural tongue. To witness this as I corn rolled Emmanuel's seven-year-old daughter Grace's hair was amazing. I looked at Cherry with tears in my eyes. We could only smile at each other, for we knew God had allowed us to be a part of something good. He allowed us to be a part of His great love. From around the world, from Rwanda, East Africa to America, a family came together...and I was there. A new family of love from the Motherland.

On the ride home, Innocent and I shared. He educates me on the massacres, children killing children, women killing women. For some reason, I only envisioned soldiers, the army killing, not lay people. I became chilled. We're talking God's goodness through all of this.

In the driveway at his home, we embraced and said goodnight. We will see each other again on Saturday night (12/21) to attend a gospel concert in West Covina. I drive off filled with joy singing *Lead Me.* I am happy.

I attempted to share the afternoon with Ernell, but to no avail. He asked if Emmanuel's parents lived in Loma Linda, and if they were Seven Day Adventist? What a response. I keep my joy and move on.

Today, at work, I continue to address ... Wait, first I must say this. On my way to work, I began to sing *Lead me, Guide me.* I sang until I believed. I cried. I began to shout with prayer, "I know my God is almighty — no evil principalities will come against me and stand. He is my Savior. I know He protects me. Heavenly Father, I call out Your name. You know my heart and my need. Four-D needs Your help. Guide us, remove the enemy who stands against us on our path. I call on Your name. I seek Your presence, Your face. I shout Hallelujah, Hallelujah. Praise the Lord. Jesus, Thank You, Jesus, Thank You, Jesus, Thank You, Jesus." I thanked Him all the way to work.

I talked with Eloise Reyes, attorney, about Riverside JTPA. She referred me to Pat Regan. Pat referred me to Mr. Albert who referred me to Mr. Shouner. He asked that I mail info to him for review. He will call me in 1-2 days after reviewing the info.

I spoke with the President of the Urban League. He thinks it may create conflict for the League since they received funds from the Riverside JTPA. He would speak with the NAACP and call me in two days.

I returned a call to my friend Jeff. He asked me, "How would I like to go to China."

I question, "China for nursing?"

"Yes."

I laughed, "Jeff, I am trying to get to Rwanda and Nigeria, I have no money."

He stops me and says, "Don't worry, how much do you need?"

"$10,000.00 for Rwanda and $7,000 for Nigeria. Who wants us in China?"

He says he has talked with "Officials" and things are getting set up and to call him after Christmas. I will make the call.

I called Cherry with the news. She responds, "I never get a man."

I reply, "We will take Celestin with us."

Tonight Dr. Curlin will call me at home after 9:00. I will continue. I must now dress to go for a Christmas tree.

12/16/96 ~ 10:00 p.m.

Well, Dr. Curlin called. I informed him of the recent events; meeting Alex Howard Bingham, letters from Minister of Health and Ms. Alice Deac, International African Bank, Emmanuel and Family. I shared our need for financial support to go to Rwanda and Nigeria. He asked that I keep him apprised of events. I requested names of individuals he felt would give us financial support. We need $10,000 for Rwanda and $7,000 for Nigeria. He said he was thinking of it. He would let me know.

12/17/96 ~ 11:00 p.m.

On my way to work, there is peace and silence. I began to sing softly *Lead me, Guide me*. Repeatedly, I sing two verses, then pray to my Heavenly Father. I am at peace. I woke up this morning at approximately 6:30 a.m. with the presence to write another letter to Ms. Christine Smith, Chief of DHS and to cc Congressman Brown. The letter from M. Martinez, dated December 9, 1996, indicated the State had reviewed the Academy's program. She is attempting to discredit the school. This letter she had not submitted to DHS or the congressman. I responded and submitted a copy of the school DHS approval. I will submit all reports to the attorney tomorrow.

Sadiq called. He's okay — back at Vacaville. He asked if I was okay, and if I was mad at him. I assured him that I was not mad and I would visit him soon.

I received a call from David Wang from the Bank of China. He asked for a copy of the school's curriculum. I explained our program. He will talk with Jeff to schedule a meeting. Jeff is real about this.

I received good financial advice today. Look at losses and find safety nets and savings. Mary Salim and I prayed today and read

Psalms 35. Powerful, powerful — it reflected my circumstance and outcome. That was my peace. God has provided me an answer to my prayers.

Well, its 11:00 p.m. Tahira is driving up. Time to chat with her.

12/18/96 ~ 7:10 a.m.

I sit on my bed reading Psalms 35: 1-28 and 37:8-28. I pray for righteousness. I seek fairness and righteousness. I pray. I began to think about the accreditation results with ABSHES. I called Chris Eaton. He says, "The letter will be sent out next week. Although I shouldn't say anything, I will say it is good. I know that will help you."

I say, "Thank you. God Bless you!" I hang up and call Cherry. I leave a message on her recorder. I hang up and cry uncontrollably — thanking Jesus.

8:45 a.m.

I am thanking Jesus. I put on Kirk Franklin and the Family. I praise the Lord. *Melodies from Heaven* and *Conquerors, Savior, More than Life, Don't Take Your Joy Away, What I think about Jesus* — I can't stop praising His name! Tears flow. I shout His name. I call Cherry and praise God into her recorder. I thank God for my life, for bringing me through the storms. I thank God for her and all she brings to the Academy and me.

I shout. I cry. I praise my Heavenly Father. I am overcome with emotion. I survived the Storm! No one but my Lord has known my pain.

Thank You, Lord. I'm alive in spirit.

12/18/96 ~ 11:00 p.m.

Oh what a day. I make it to work feeling cleansed and healed. I don't know what tomorrow will bring, but right now is all that matters. I work on the information for attorney Nicholas Schobiten. It's delivered by 4:30 p.m.

I called Howard Bingham (Muhammad Ali's friend) and leave a message. I need his address to invite him to our Christmas party. He returns my call from Detroit. He provides me with his address in Los Angeles. I ask if he had any progress with our 'package,' and he says it's coming along. He then informs me that he is in Detroit. Muhammad Ali lives in Detroit. I call Cherry and she tells me Forstin, Celestin's brother who had gone to Ali's ranch, is meeting someone in Detroit. Could it be Howard?

I called Jeff to discuss China. He updates me on what is desired. He has spoken to David Wang of Asian Pacific Investments. We plan to meet Jan. 2nd or 3rd, 1997. I call David and brief him on the conversation I had with Jeff. He and I look forward to the meeting. I called Cherry to notify her of the meeting as well. In the meantime, I received a call from Celestin via Cherry.

He and I discussed the Genocide Conference in 1998. We wish to have the President of Rwanda as a guest speaker. Also, Don Bell wants to meet the President of Rwanda University. Celestin has his work cut out. He requests we also ask the President of the country to attend the conference.

A busy day ends with having dinner with my dear friend Tamara Ambroson, affectionately called "Ms. T."

I'm tired. Goodnight.

12/22/96 ~ 12:20 p.m.

Robert Rochelle said we would be International. So did Aisha, my baby. They were right.

God, I prayed. Now I must be open and prepared to receive your blessing.

Cherry and I marvel at Your work. We marvel at our endless energy and love for what we do. Thank You for bringing us together.

Love, Your Worker

Through God, all things are possible.

12/24/96 ~ 7: 35 a.m.

I awake at 6:00 a.m., dress, and go to Wal-Mart for last-minute gifts for my nephews. As I look into the mirror, I look different...smaller. I smile. My imagination runs wild. No weight lost here. As I drive down Benson, I look over the valley below. The lights all aglow. Peace, peace, peace. I smile in the presence of the Lord. I think of the last 12 hours. I can't ask, Why me? I can only say thank you. I know this is God's process. It is good. At work, I kneel and pray. I can't cry. I ask the Lord to keep me humbled and focused on Four-D. I pray for the continued opportunity to make a positive difference in someone's life.

I think of Cherry and the excitement of the Academy, her desire to quit the County. Four-D and I are blessed. I ask God to provide us what we need to continue to say, "Through God, all things are possible."

8:15 a.m.

I call Cherry and tell her Nigeria is out. We make a spiritual pact as friends and Sisters. I will not allow her to ever forget our purpose. She must always remain level-headed. She excitedly discussed the Academy, printing shop, goals, the business, and her desire to quit her county job.

We agree that Celestin should be here for Saturday's celebration of Friends of Four-D success Academy.

My God, My God, thank You. Your Child, Linda

12/24/96 ~ 3:45 p.m.

Today we graduated seven students. Large or small, we fulfill the desires to help make a difference in someone's life. We were blessed by Kimberly Pauley, a wonderful voice in song. We shared briefly after the ceremony. I reminded her of my statement 7-8 months ago at a graduation of going through the valley. But I rejoice in knowing God is bringing me up to the mountaintop.

Her husband had it in his heart to have Shelly deliver this message to me. "He who took me through the valley will bring me out!" From this awesome word, 1997 is going to be big and moving! Yes, I know he is right. I have been told he will be in my office at 12:00 noon on December 26, 1996. I will be here.

Happy Holiday and God Bless to us all.

12/26/96 ~ 12:04 p.m.

I picked up a chocolate cake at 7:45 this morning from Cherry. It is for Bill. As we stood on her front porch, we both agreed that if for nothing else we have dreamed of all the things we would like the business to be. They made us <u>dream.</u> If we have been hallucinating, it's the best yet.

I sit here doing a day's productive work. I must continue on regardless of all hopes and dreams. Four-D Success Academy is Real!

Press on! Thank You, Jesus for this day.

12/30/96 ~ 9:10

My friend Jeff is still working on his financial freedom.

Yesterday, I was thinking about all that is going on with me, my life, and the school. It finally hit me that God has created an opportunity for me. Why should I doubt Him? If I had not had trust in Jeff, my dearest friend, how could he be willing to give to me so freely?

I asked Jeff if he was the "Second Coming?" He laughed and states, "God is real."

I later called Jeff to acknowledge my thoughts. I told him where I wanted to place a school and I wait for approval. I thank him for his friendship. I again felt peace. We parted.

Innocent attended church with Aisha and I. He later said it was the first time he had felt and seen the spirit of God move through the church. The minister was preaching and people were talking and praising God. He sees men crying. It was a good feeling for him. At my home, he and I ate dinner and talked for several hours about his home and the tragedy. His presence enlightens me. His story saddens me, but I gained knowledge of the area I desired to travel to.

Today, we received the written notice of 'Accreditation' from ABHES. As soon as possible for Financial Aid. Got to be approved in 60 days.

God is good. Thank You, Lord.

1/2/97 ~ 6:33 p.m.

Today Cherry Houston, Celestin Semuhungu, and I met with David Wang of Asia Pacific Investment. We (CLS International Consultants) discussed Four-D Success Academy providing Nursing Education.

We were well-received. David asked how soon we could go. I was thinking March. He was talking this month or February.

We have committed to Rwanda for early February. Therefore, it was agreed to go February 20th for two weeks.

We are going to Beijing, China to meet with individuals in the Department of Education and Department of Health. We will tour 2-3 providences. There are 30 providences in China. Mr. Wang would like FDSA in each. God will allow us to serve the masses! Mr. Wang will call me next week.

After the meeting, Cherry, Celestin, and I had a prayer. We are so thankful to God for this opportunity.

Thank You, Lord.

1/10/97 ~ 10:25 a.m.

We are now accredited by Accrediting Bureau Health Education Schools! God, thank You. The only African-American Accredited Nursing School.

I made a presentation to the Riverside Workforce Board, addressing the false allegations against the school by M. Martinez. God was with me. My spirit was at peace. I spoke, and they listened. I only seek the truth. Justice will prevail. The Urban League has a meeting with Pat Ramos (Riv. Sup). I had a long discussion with Jeff about my situation. I was honest and direct. If supported, I would take action.

The LVN Board will be reviewing us next week. I know all is well. Cherry is truly an excellent Director. She is focused, knowledgeable, organized, and on top of things.

We met with David Wang (Cherry, Celestin and I) last week. I am awaiting a call from him. We may be going to China. On Saturday, January 18th, Cherry and I will be going to Washington, DC for the President's Inauguration Ball. Her sister's church choir will be singing.

We are planning our trip to Rwanda for February 3rd – 15th. We (Cherry and I, Celestin and Don) are excited about the possibilities of helping others.

I spoke with Pastor John in Nigeria. I am in a dilemma on whether to go or not. God, protect us. If funds are available, Cherry and I may go.

Funds. Lord knows, at this time the account is $16,000+ but He has all. Stay focused, faithful, truthful. All is okay.

Thank You, Jesus for the staff and support.

1/16/97 ~ 7:00 p.m.

Marcia Peterson, Consultant from the LVN Board, completed her three-day review. Thanks to God, all went well. We will receive our Accreditation. Cherry will request to have 20 students enrolled in April and 30 students enrolled in April and 30 in June.

She will also submit a new schedule for a 10-month program in April. We have truly been blessed. I have an appointment in the morning in Carlsbad. I will be meeting with T. Jones to discuss the application for financial aid. The goal is to have the LVN and the upcoming Pharmacy Technician programs approved for funding. Lord, this will truly make a difference. Less reliance upon JTPA for funds.

I am truly trying to market the Intravenous (IV) and Dir. of Staff Development (DSD) classes. Low enrollments but I pray for 15 per class.

After Marcia left, the staff present stood together and prayed. We are so thankful to God for the blessings He has given us.

I received a call earlier this week from the Black Chamber of Commerce. I was nominated for Business Person of the Year. I follow God's lead.

1/23/97 ~ 12:20 a.m.

Last Saturday, Cherry and I traveled to Washington, DC with the praise singers of the Church of Christ. The group was invited to sing at the 53rd Inaugural Ball for President Clinton and Vice President Al Gore. It was a wonderful experience. We attended three churches on Sunday, and the choir sang for His Excellency, Dr. Theogene Rudasinga of Rwanda. He was moved and appreciated all efforts and support to Rwanda.

Cherry and I met with him on Tuesday, January 22nd, and discussed our upcoming trip to Rwanda (2/3 - 2/15) and the needs of the country. At the conclusion of our meeting, we invited him to California. He accepted and tentatively scheduled to be here April 15,

1997. He will visit Four-D Success Academy, L.A., Cal Poly Pomona, and UC Davis, along with other sites. Much planning is ahead.

I was selected as the 1st runner up to receive the Business Person of the Year award from the Black Chamber of Commerce.

We continue to strive towards excellence. Today, in Shirley's class, all seven students received 100% on medical terminology test. They will strive to excel and have perfect attendance.

God will guide us. Thank You, Lord.

1/26/97 ~ 7:00 p.m.

Today has been a truly blessed day. I am overwhelmed by God's spirit.

Aisha (my daughter) and I attended the 7:30 a.m. service at Loveland. What a blessed surprise, she joined the church. She acknowledged the Lord and Savior Jesus Christ. I couldn't stop crying.

We then attended the 11:00 a.m. service at Victory Community Church with Pastors Tommy and Gloria Morrow. Pastor Morrow preached and taught on believing in God and believing God. In believing in God, we know He can. In believing God, we know He will. It is our Faith in His ability to do all things. I am just floating internally and externally with tears. Aisha and I returned to the Chapel at 5:00 p.m. for her baptism. Lord, what a blessing to witness my second child accept Jesus Christ.

We (Cherry, Don Bell, Celestin and I) are scheduled to fly to Rwanda Africa on February 3, 1997. I must, at this time, charge the trip, but I know God will make a way.

Last week, I was selected as 1st runner up as Business Person of the Year by the Black Chamber of Commerce. I have not taken the time to stop and reflect on the past twelve months. God, keep us together forever. Your child and Four-D Success Academy, Inc.

1/29/97 ~ 5:32 p.m.

Today, Charlie Seymour and I represented Four-D Success Academy in Small Claims. Dameron Communications had filed a claim for $200. The judgment was ruled in the Academy's favor. Dameron was found in breach of contract when he did not pay the Academy's bills timely.

Cherry and I are scheduled to leave Saturday, February 1, 1997. We have run into some financial difficulties, but I (we) stand firm that God will provide. He creates the path for us to travel. I am awaiting the approval for the loan from commerce Bank of California for $150,000. It's in God's Hands.

1/31/97 ~ 4:25 a.m.

I have worked through the night, completing tasks. I must do all that I can for Four-D before I leave for Rwanda.

2/1/97 ~ 9:30 p.m.

We're off on British Airways to London, Ethiopia, then on to Rwanda. I sit here with the song of Whitney Houston, *He's all over me and He's keeping me alive.* God is our guide. I prayed as we took off. We fly on the wings of Jesus we are safe. This flight is great. A menu was passed out with selections of: smoked salmon, roasted herb chicken or mix grilled meats, filet, turkey, ham, raspberry crumble, cheese, coffee and tea. Two movies: *A Time to Kill* and *The First*

Wives Club. Complimentary drinks and Continental breakfast to come. And guess what, we're in coach! What is First Class receiving?

Leaving home was different. I will be gone for two weeks and I don't know how much I will miss not being home. Aisha helped me pack, Tahira worried about grocery shopping and whether or not her dad would sign a check so that she could shop. She decided to pay for everything (including Aisha's needs), and I would be reimbursing her when I returned. Ernell and I did our 'cheek' thing. That, I will not miss! He seems very disinterested in all that I do. I know life has changed for us, yet my sadness is replaced with joy. I am going to seek out my extended mission. This is part of God's plan.

I went to the office today to pray. I could not leave Four-D Success Academy without kneeling in my office to ask God to watch over it, the staff, and our finances. I prayed for peace at work and home. I prayed for our safe journey. I prayed that we be of assistance and of service to those we were going to see. I prayed for me!

We are off. God, I thank You for this blessing and friends.

Cherry, Don, and Linda Smith

2/1/97 ~ 7:40 a.m.

Well, we left London yesterday. It was a pleasure meeting Helen Scmahunga and Vickie Mutaboba. We were treated hospitably. We are having a good time. We have just landed at Asmara, Ethiopia.

The landing strip. As I look out the window, I only see dirt, shrubs and, yes, the airport. We will have a two-hour layover before heading to our final destination: Addis Ababa, Ethiopia.

2/4/97 ~ 12:10 p.m.

We are aboard the airline leaving Ethiopia and heading to Kigali Rwanda. We had a great time visiting Joseph Mutaboba, 1st Consult of Ethiopia. Yesterday, we visited the Museum. I found out who "Lucy" is (was). The bones of a female believed to be 3.5 million years old. She stood 3½ ft. walked on 2 feet. I learned about the Axien, a 24 ft. granite cut rock with design.

I saw artifacts inside of a great hut. Joseph and I consumed a bottle of Ethiopian red wine. We all visited the American Embassy and I met Michael Brenner, Ambassador. We visited the Rwanda Embassy and the Ambassador. We went to a restaurant and had _more_ wine. I was so tired and mellow that Cherry asked me not to speak because I was incoherent!

We returned to Joseph's home and ate more food. I had soup and they ate beans, rice, beef, and salad. I retired, unable to hold my head up any longer.

This morning, we had bread, butter, jelly, grapefruit, papaya, and chicken wieners with coffee, and fresh squeezed orange juice.

We discussed the criteria for candidates for the Rwanda Education Project, and the make-up of the committee.

Celestin is having some difficulties.

2/5/97 ~ 1:00 a.m.

We had an afternoon of sharing and visiting. I spent two hours with Caritas at her shop and beauty supply store, walking with her husband Alfred. Upon our return, we all sat around a table in the busy room chattering. Everyone: Cherry, Don, Phillis (Godmother of Helen from London), Clementine who is getting married on

Saturday, 2/10/97, Louise, Tobe, Alfred, and Curtis. At about 9 p.m. Cherry, Don, and I left to attend a dinner held so we could meet others. We were joined by Celestine and Annewho operated a support group for women and orphans. Anne was the assistant to the Minister of the Health of Kantengwa, Louis, Christian Utomin.

What a lovely dinner, with wine and coffee. At 12:07, we left to return to Caritas home. What a wonderful night. We discussed the needs of the Rwandese, education, teacher training, plumes, electricians, merchants, high technology, etc.

I ask God to allow us to be of service...Don, Cherry, and I, and all those who wish to join us.

Let Four-D Success Academy be of service in having funds, staff, and no problem with prayers.

As always, guide us ALL, Lord. Your Faithful Child, Linda

I've yet to call home. I can't call from Caritas's home. I will call tomorrow.

2/6/97

It's early, the time I don't know. The roosters started calling early. I guess it was sunrise. I lay quietly and I hear drums beating faintly rhythmically in a far off distance. They beat and beat. I hear a faint humming song and sounds with the drums. The drumming and singing stops, the roosters still call. Someone is up walking outside. I think today will be a good day. Cherry is asleep and I think of Celestin Semuhungu coming home and a tear forms. I am happy and I look forward to his family reunion at the airport.

2/6/1997 ~ 9:30 a.m.

I walked the grounds this morning. The helpers are cleaning, gardening, washing, propping, preparing breakfast.

Breakfast - Coffee, tea, sweet bread, fresh pineapples, papaya, bananas, mango, butter, jam. I ate until I was content. Then Caritas insisted I have another slice of papaya.

Next to the house is a brick wall with barbed wire. We're told criminals of the Genocide are kept there. 8,000. Today we travelled to where Celestin lived as a boy.

11:09 a.m.

I stand beside the house, praying as the sun bathes my skin. I pray to God and thank Him for the presence of my heart. I look at the gardener, the flowers, the red dirt, the chickens. I stand on African soil. I am home, comfortable. I am at peace. There is something tranquil about this place. The pace is slower, no rush. Things happen as they should.

I stand at the entrance to the yard, greeting those passing by. "Aiahee", a soldier, walks by with a gun to his side. He seems to be a young man, no more than 20. I watch him pass me by seemingly unnoticed.

Don and Cherry are working on scheduling appointments.

I miss home. I haven't been able to call because the house telephone is for local calls only. I'll call this evening between 6-8 p.m. At home it should be between 8-10 a.m. We're off for the day.

2/7/97 ~ 1:26 a.m.

Oh what a day it was. We traveled to Alfred and Caritas's business home about 1½ hours away, stopping for pictures. What a lovely place with 10 rooms and gardens. We ate and continued our journey to the site of the genocide at the Church of the Invitation. Over 100,000 people were murdered. The memorial gravesites mark where thousands rest. We entered into the Church. What an awesome feeling to know they went there for prayer and refuge, yet they died, all of them.

We obtained permission to see an area behind locked doors. The skeleton, skulls, bones are embedded in my mind. People laid dead...old dusty clothing and bones caked with dust. I see dusty red plants, skeletal lower extremities, and no upper body. We were told by the guard that his parents' bones were in the rubble. After the killings, the murderers threw hand grenades into the crowd to make sure all were dead. We cried and prayed. A very solemn period. We left there, never to be the same again.

Today, I received a new name: Umuhoza= Comforter of the People.

Cherry's new name is Umutesi, which means Well-kept Woman from Early On.

We visited the speaker of the Parliament, Juvenile, and his wife, Artisia.

We returned home. Caritas gave her husband Alfred permission to marry me! She was serious. He offered two cows and a night with me. I declined. Bedtime alone.

2/9/97 ~ 7:40 a.m.

I lost track of the date, but I know it's Friday morning. Tomorrow is the BIG DAY — the wedding for Clementine. Yesterday, we traveled with Father Oreste Incimatataya, a young man and dear friend (school mate) of Celestin Semuhungu. We went to see his school: Don Bosco Institute in "Brumenco". He is building dormitories for girls and boys, classrooms, tablets, and kitchen area. He will start with 43 females and 37 males. Of this population, 47 of them will be orphans. His work has been the work of God. He has raised the funds through his own donations for his job as Priest, through the Catholic Charities, Caritas's Orphanages, and from others. Therefore he has provided from all sources $60,000 and he needs more.

From the school we went to a market place. What an experience. Residents selling dry goods, clothing. We were followed by a crippled, mentally incompetent young boy. Other begging children gathered around us, seeming to encourage him on. Finally, some adults disbursed the crowd, but the begging child continued to follow us for some time. We took many pictures. I found some of the residents turning away or running, for they didn't want to be captured on film. Father Oreste returned to the market place to pick us up.

From there, we went to eat. We dined on chicken, potatoes, and salad. Father Oreste had to bring us home for he had much to do. He is leaving Sunday for Europe for three weeks. He is somewhat concerned about the school opening on time. I dreamed it opened. I could see boys looking out the door windows.

Celestin will not be here. He is having difficulty with his passport in the U.S. We are all saddened. Cherry who has been waiting for him in Rwanda, has a saddened look on her face. She is comforted by those around her with hugs and word to comfort her. The evening turned to joy; we ate a great meal at 10:30 p.m. then partied and danced until 3 a.m.

We all danced, child, young, and older. Phillis danced nonstop (age 73) and even had to change clothes. Don danced. We had a grand time. Don is a true delight. He was somewhat disappointed when we stopped at 3:00 a.m.

Life is good. Cherry and I reflect on our new names and their meanings.

I don't see Cherry's name Umutesi being about her, as much as it is about those around her and the loving care she gives to others.

Our experience is unexplainable. Alfred still wishes to marry me. Last night, I asked (jokingly) if he could take care of me and he adamantly said, "Yes."

Laughing, I said "And when the next pretty lady comes along, you will have another new wife."

He looks lovingly at me and says, "No, you will be my last." I've heard these words before from another. I think of him and Alfred and smile.

Everyone is up early, cleaning. Today, we meet with the Minister of Health to review (I hope) the curriculum, and to see at least one hospital. We did see one Nursing School from the outside yesterday in our travels with Father Orestes. It was quite large.

Time to dress for the day.

11:35 p.m.

We visited the school and discussed the current nursing programs. I desired changes. Everything with the program seems new: Nursing and Physiotherapy are three-year programs which started one month ago. Patient Aide is a six-month program in its fourth month. The nursing school trained 500 aides this year.

We attended Clementine and Albert's civil wedding ceremony. The room was hot and crowded with 20-30 couples and friends. The minister read instructions, provided advice, and then each couple was sworn in by saying vows, raising their right hand. First the man, and then the woman. After completing the vows, the witness signed the book and each couple returned to their seat. This process continued until every couple present had taken their oath. After the ceremony the couples were greeted by well wishes before going their separate ways.

1) If the couples were to have a religious ceremony, then the male and female went to their own homes. They are reunited with the religious ceremony. The religious ceremony can take place within 24 hours up to one year.

2) If the couple chose not to have a religion ceremony, then they can go home together.

3) If the couple does not come together after the civil ceremony, then they may choose to divorce.

Cherry has worked with Mutsindashyaka Theoneste, the Deputy Minister in internal affairs. Cherry is giving Valentine English lessons. The BIG DAY is tomorrow. Goodnight.

2/9/97 ~ 11:58 p.m.

The Wedding took place on 2/8/97. Hustle and bustle. The house was filled with guests and workers preparing for the ceremony to begin at the house. The patio was set with rugs, tables and chairs. The groom's and bride's families set on opposite sides of the room with the bride and groom in the center.

The groom's father or representative had to convince the bride's father or representative that his son was worthy of having his daughter. So the storytelling began, the goal for the groom's father to respond to questions suitably to the bride's father. The bride's father says, "Clementine was sick and they had to take her to the hospital, on the way the car broke down. Alfred's family drove by very quickly and didn't offer to help. If they couldn't stop when she was sick, why do they think the family would care for her now?"

The groom's father responded with, "My car was so dirty and Clementine was so sick. I know my car would make her worse. I would not do that again."

The bride's father said he had to get a taxi to take Clementine to the hospital…the groom's father said he knew, for he paid for the taxi. Clementine's father doesn't believe him but the young man hosting the event says it is true. They paid for the taxi… Clementine's father says he's not sure that the young man is telling the truth, but since he is a family member of Clementine, he must believe him.

Each father gives an acceptance speech and exchanges gifts. Now the groom's father asks for Clementine for his son, but Clementine's father says she will be ready on February 8th, in one year.

They have plenty of food, so the groom's family can stay and visit. They love Clementine so, but she is so young she needs time.

The groom's father says his son is young and he played with Clementine when she was young. Now they can grow up together, besides, Clementine's younger sisters want to marry his other sons.

Clementine's father says that the groom must give a gift. The groom's father replied he would not come so far without a gift. He brought a cow. The cow is brought up to the driveway. A longhorn brown beautiful cow is presented. A man set leaves before the cow and lit a fire. He began to sing a song and dance for the cow and Clementine. After the presentation, we all ate and drank before going to the Church for the religious ceremony. The bride and groom change into European traditional clothing. The Church ceremony is done by Father Orestes.

After the Church ceremony, there was much more to come. We went to the reception where several hundred people gathered.

The ceremony had singing, dancing, and drinks from the pot. We were called by the announcer to come forward and drink. We were introduced as the new Rwanda family members. Everyone ate, drank, and gave gifts to the bride and groom. After 4-5 hours, we went to the groom and bride's house to drink for 1 hour, then we returned to Caritas's house at about 9:30 p.m. where many gather for more talk and drink at 11:00 p.m. Caritas had food for us to eat. I was totally exhausted yet everyone was now preparing for the after-party, which started at midnight. I was so sleepy I was asked to go to bed. The others went to the party until 3 a.m.

Today, we were with Minister Joseph Nsengimana, Minister of Higher Education, and Alex. We went to Ymatata, a site of genocide. We past a field lined with crosses, some with names of the dead. At the Church, we were told how the men left to fight. The militia soldiers came and killed all the women and children. They threw hand grenades into the Church. A memorial now stands with multiple shelves displaying the skulls and bones of the dead — both adults and babies. I cried. I don't understand how this could happen. Joseph's wife and children all died in the genocide. We left there and went to another Church known as the 'hog of bones'. Hundreds were killed there. Their bones are now in bags. A large grave is dug inside and the bones will be placed there. The Church will never be used again, but it will be a place where all people can come to remember. In the back of the Church a large grave is being dug for the hundreds of bodies that were bulldozed into a ditch! The Monks wanted to give them a proper burial.

We left the burial and went to visit the school that Joseph and Alex operate. Joseph was one of 84 teachers, teaching 460 students. The genocide killed all but 12 teachers and 100 students. The school is operated as intended to educate Rwandan children. When the Rwandans were relocated there by the Government, the children were not allowed to enter secondary level training. So the 84 parents started their own school. *Control the mind of the people, and you control the behavior of the people.* We visited the dormitory where the boys and girls stayed. The kids sleep 10 to a room on floor mats. It cost $200-300 a year per child. Teachers are limited, so volunteers come on Saturdays to help.

2/10/97 ~ 10:07 a.m.

We returned to Caritas's house to prepare for the gathering at Clementine's and Albert's house. Everyone gathered at the entrance of the gate, holding baskets filled with gifts. After the "Chairman" Clementine's father entered, we all followed in a line to deliver the gifts. After all of the gifts were delivered, several people went into the house to unveil the newlyweds. They were covered with white cloth. Once removed, they were given milk to drink. They, in turn, gave milk to the children to drink. The husband cut the hair of his wife. This symbolizing the traditional hair carving the Rwandan women were to do. The couple fed all the guests, and then we left. This ceremony now allows the couple to leave their home for Activities of Daily Living (ADL) and to visit others.

What a day. Alex offered me land – a home. He called me last night to ask me out for an evening. If my schedule allows, I will go.

The African air is romantic. I am pleased and overwhelmed at how everyone accepts me. Until I speak, the Rwandan people think I am one of them – not a US Citizen. I do look Rwandese.

2/12/97

I didn't have my diary on Tuesday. So here is a note of our experience. I had the opportunity to visit the Pediatric room of a hospital, the "poor" hospital. The conditions were appalling. 2-3 babies with their mothers were on cots. A woman was washing dirty dishes in dirty water at her bedside. Empty soda bottles were about the dirty floor, and the walls needed cleaning. IV bottles unlabeled. There were needles left in bottles in the med room. Cabinets left unlocked, partially open sterile packages. No suitable equipment to work with. The baby I visited had drop foot, contractures of the hand. Congested, but no Gemco or suctioning equipment available. Oxygen not on, I don't even know if the tank had any oxygen in it. No feeding tube noted. A one-year-old infant appeared to be 7-8 months. Crying, I became very anxious about the need to assist in correcting these issues.

There must be a higher standard by which the nursing staff consciously operates to promote the quality of life of the patients.

I eagerly waited to meet the Minister of Health Dr. Komera to discuss Health Care and Nursing Education.

This evening (last night), we had dinner with Dr. Vincent Biruta and friends at a local restaurant. Chicken, fries, salad, beer, and martinis. What a delightful evening. Cherry, Don, Phillis, and I had a ball. When I leave, I will miss much.

Celestin will be here Saturday the 15th. I am thinking of staying until Tuesday. I would hate to miss him and the action of his work along with Cherry. I am a part of CLS International. Home is fine, I guess. I've not talked with anyone but Aisha. They have the number to call me and I informed them that I did not have access to a telephone so I could not call home. Caritas's phone is only for local calls. With the time difference (10 hrs.) when I am awake home is asleep. 12 noon in USA = 10-11 p.m. here.

2/12/97 ~ 9:35 a.m.

We have a 9:30 appt with Dr. Komera. Cherry and I concluded that everyone adjusted to the late time. Our driver is here at 10:00 a.m. Now we wait for Don Bell to finish getting dressed. He decided to accompany us since his meeting was cancelled.

2/13/97

Yesterday was not a good day for me. I was disgusted with the cancelled appointments. The mayor spoke at the Stadium and the entire town closed. There were 20,000 at the Stadium. All civil employees and citizens. People were sitting around, listening to the radio. The speech started at 9:00 a.m. and ended at 3:00 p.m. We did hold our committee meeting with Dr. Jean Bisco, Birlara, Caritas, Louise Don, Cherry, and I. Progress was made on the criteria for admission. We also visited the Ethiopian Travel to confirm and change flight time. Don is leaving this Saturday, 2/15. I decided to stay until the 22nd with Cherry. But after our visit with Ussif and Joy, I thought about leaving. I felt so overwhelmed not hearing from home, not hearing from the office. I was concerned about finances, depressed over the condition of Health Care. Cherry is about sick of me today (yesterday) and didn't mind if I left. She told me to get rid of the attitude, that we are making progress.

I received a call from Aisha while I was sitting in Caritas's room praying and crying, asking God to keep me focused and to trust in Him in taking care of Four-D Success Academy. My baby lifted my spirit. She informed me she had volunteered to work at Pomona Valley Medical Center. I am so pleased with her focus. She said "something" told her to go there. God guides her. Her father refuses to support her in my absence with spending money. I am grateful she has my gas card to get to and from school. We talked about school, application of time for success, Church, me here in Africa, my concerns and joy while here.

I told her I would stay if the school was okay. So I had her connect me with Pam and Frankie. Frankie had to pull $8,000 from Wells

Fargo. She feels comfortable about the finances. She will call Ernell if necessary to sign checks. Pam has had contact with the Council about proper renewal. They can't locate the check so she will place a hold and receive another. Pam feels all is well and is comfortable with me staying another week. I then had Aisha call Charlie to attend the meeting next Tuesday with the Committee for Ambassador Rudasinga. He agreed, and I felt so much better after speaking with Aisha. I love her dearly.

Today, we met with Prosper Higiro, the Minister of Commerce. We Discussed International Trade, Agriculture, Sports, and Business Development.

We met with Dr. Vincent Biruta, Minister of Health. We discussed Nursing Service and financial support. He seemed very receptive. We also met Dr. Charles Rudakubana, Director of Cabinet. We have a dinner appointment with them next Tuesday.

Last night, Charles Ngarambe took us out for socialization. We had a nice time laughing, talking, and having wine. I met a gentleman named Major John. He is an attorney who joined the Rwandan Patriotic Front (RPF) to fight the war.

This evening, we are to have a marble tournament. I am declaring victory – more to come. Oh yes, I also spoke with Harriette Baledro. She's a nurse who helps revise the A2 Nurse curriculum.

She gave us hope and lifted my spirits! We will meet with her tomorrow with Dr. Rantegrob and Mary, Director of Nurses.

2/14/97 ~ 7:25 a.m.

I am surprised I am up so early after last night. We were taken out to dinner by Theoneste and Dornatele to a restaurant. Caritas, Alfred, Musafi, Cherry, Don, and I feasted on beef, roasted chicken, fish, chips, beer and wine. We had a great time. We were later joined by Robert Ford. The young TV Producer who is assisting with footage for the Rwanda Education Project. He and I had a good intellectual discussion on slavery, the genocide, and education. He invited us out tonight. There is a great deal of excitement of the possibilities of development in all areas: Technology, Health Care Industry, Education, Trade, and Redevelopment. The sky is the limit.

Yesterday, Theoneste told me that someone told him a Rwandan woman speaking fluent English was seen in the bank. He told that person I was from Uganda and had learned English there. We had a good laugh. I am surprised of the correlation of my features with the Rwandan.

Today is Valentine's Day. No calls will be coming this way and none sent out. I hope to get my hair done today and find a bank that will cash my Travelers Check.

2/15/97 ~ 7:55

I did get a call from home. Aisha had told her dad of my plight. I need money, about $200. I found out I will need $60-70 to get out of the Country. I told Ernell I would call, but Don Bell loaned me $200. Hopefully, Ernell will call back since it is difficult and costly for me to call home.

Don Bell left today. I was sad to see him go. He is such a delight. He took many artifacts home. Witch Doctor masks, dolls, baskets, cloth.

He will share them with shops in hope that they will purchase more from Rwanda.

Celestin Semuhungu came home today after 15-17 years. He returned to his family. Cherry and I are joyful for many reasons. We are grateful that God allowed us to play a small part in his homecoming. His sister, Caritas, is quiet but I know her joy is inexpressible. At the house, she began to talk and laugh with him and Alfred. It was a pure joy to witness this family reunion.

Celestin is here to work. He has already been on the telephone with Vincent Biruta to directly discuss our financial needs to continue our work in Education here.

I am happy to be here this week. It would have been a mistake for me to leave. I thank God for taking care of Four-D Success Academy. I thank God for what He has allowed Four-D Success Academy to contribute to others in an unselfish way. I am thankful that God provided the funds for this trip, that He paid the bills at home and work. I know He will take care of all things. I am thankful for my heart to love and share, and my willingness to contribute to others.

This evening we will go out for dance, laughter, and fun, as guest of Charles.

Charlie called to say hi, and to inquire as to why Cherry and I didn't come down today. He also informed me he was going on the Peter Jennings show in New York. He had received a call from his niece. The show is interested in him doing a segment on "Solutions". He has received 40-60 computer desks. Charlie's computer program has taken off. I look forward to seeing him again.

2/16/97 ~ 12:55 a.m.

Last night Charlie, Cherry, Celestin, and I were taken to the Cadillac Club. It was designed very nice. The Dance floor is in the center. We went straight to the floor and danced until we (I) got tired. The music was nonstop. We arrived at 10:45/11:00 p.m. Charles said it would get busy at 1:00 a.m. By 12:30 a.m. the place was filling up. The dance floor had people dancing that I don't think even sat down. The relationship and freedom to dance was most different. Different men and women, same sex, all enjoyed dancing. At one point, a young man grabbed my hand, swinging me around and began dancing.

My partner Charles didn't skip a beat. He joined me and we had a ball. I was wet, hot, tired, and full of fun. Cherry and Celestin looked like puppies in love. She just radiated all evening. She looked extremely exotic with her beautiful smile under the light. I could tell that she and Celestin are in love. Even Charles said it and smiled about what he had witnessed. Celestin was so tired that at 12 his head was almost in Cherry's lap. We (I) suggested we go, he said at 1 a.m. He revived himself and we all danced until 1:30 a.m.

Charles is a smooth and good dancer. I appreciate the time he has shared with us. Today, I showed Musafe how to make a grilled cheese sandwich. They were big hits. We made 7 for breakfast. Since we had butter, bread, and cheese, every morning, I decided to do something different. Introduced a bit of America. Clementine and Albert are to be here today at 3:30 for a small celebration. It's been a week since the wedding.

Musafe passed his secondary test. He is now a graduate of High School. Next is his enrollment into the University. Cherry and I discussed all the possibilities of service. We desire to function as Consultants to the Nursing Department. There is a great deal of training needed – to train the instructors on delivery. There are some instructors who are not nurses teaching nursing subjects. There is no tier system in the hospital, no supervisors, or charge nurse. Possible lack of accountability. I wish to introduce the Quality Assurance Process.

I continue to think of the baby at the hospital. There is something about the Hydrogen tank (O2) that bothered me. Then I realized I didn't see a humidifier or regulator on the tank! I could tell at a glance if it was on or off. I was so concerned about the infant's foot drop and the gauge in the mouth. I almost had a medical shut down. My mind became so boggled with thoughts. There is so much to do.

2/18/97 ~ 5:07 p.m.

I didn't enter yesterday. After visiting the hospital, I felt sick. The odor, the lack of nursing processes in ALL areas. Patients with TB not in isolation. Urine pan filled on the floor, inadequate H2O, 2-3 babies per bed, mothers in bed with babies, poor nutritional diets, unidentified licensed staff, unskilled and lacking a theory process. I know that God has sent us here with hearts of compassion filled with care to help improve what we can. I pray that He controls the thoughts I think and the words I speak. I pray that Dr. Komera finds favor in us, in our efforts, and in our ability. I pray for a contract (5 years) for CLS International Consulting Services. I know He will help us locate the resources needed to help Rwanda.

Last evening, we were taken out by John Baptiste (I had previously met him in Detroit) for a dinner of chicken, banana, beer, wine, and fries. This food is GOOD!

We returned home at 10:45 and Caritas asked if we would eat something. She is a jewel. I must leave something special for her. She likes the red two-piece casual set. It's hers.

Today, we met with Alice and Caritas to discuss the REP Committee. She will function as a consultant, if needed. While Celestin met with Dr. Vincent Biruta, Cherry and I received a driver named Ollie. He was a delight. He spoke English, took us shopping, and bargained for us. He gave Cherry another name, "Umamahoaro" which means God placed her (in this world) for peace. She screamed with delight for this fit her well. "Umamahoaro Umetesi." We brought "Igisabo," butter makers, and other pleasurable items. Today was a good day. Tonight at 6:30, we are going out with Dr. Charles and Dr. Vincent. I expect a pleasant and charming evening.

2/19/97 ~ 4:40 p.m.

Last evening seemed to be the best. Cherry, Celestin, Vincent, Charles, Fillipian, Caritas, Alfred, Louise, Cathy, and I met at a restaurant for drinks and food. We laughed until I cried. English, French, and Rwandan were being spoken at the table. Translation was going around the table. Cherry and I consumed a bottle of wine, while Louise and Charles chose Brandy and beer. The others had wine. I don't enter this to discuss the alcohol, but to remind me of an evening of laughter, and friendship building over the evening with beverages. When the chicken and bananas came, it was more than we could eat. I was amazed of how delicious and satisfying a simple meal is. We spoke of life in Rwanda, and Cherry inquired about homosexuality. Charles said it does not exist. Homosexuality (same sex relations) is a European ideal. The open expression of the culture to hold hands and embrace each other totally defies America culture. I've seen soldiers walking with guns strapped to their shoulders, walking and holding hands. Women and children all participate in this culturally accepted display of kinship. I have yet to witness any sexual connotation displayed between the same sex. The culture is beautiful, we agreed. I asked to go dancing on Friday. Charles is taking us out for Saturday. Cherry and I must journey home. I/we know much awaits us. I was told that Pam called after we left last evening. I mentally began to question: what was the reason for the call? Then I thought I'm better off thinking she called with good news, for bad news now would do me no good. I entered into the room and Cherry told me not to even start. She heard the message. She verbalized what was going through my mind. I had nothing to say!

Today was the big day to meet with Dr. Komera, Minister of Health, at 9:00 a.m.

As we entered into his office, I was moved and pleased. He is an attractive young man. I feel all of the members who are nursing the country appear to be between 35-45 years of age. The President is 47. Dr. Komera received us well. He discussed the current situations of Rwanda, the cause of the genocide. Colonists try to take over and rule the country, divide and conquer. The need for education in all areas with support and contacts. He made contact with a Medical Training School to help assist the 129 physicians in the country. We discussed services and training. I spoke on quality, professionalism, and performance. I assured Dr. Komera if he gave me the financial support we needed, we would provide our very best. He asked what it would take to bring me back to Rwanda. I told him

I would need a budget, and a contract to do the service. He was open, said he could find the money. He requested that we submit a plan with a budget to him. He said we need not worry about housing, ground transportation, or a building. CLS International members have been well-received in Rwanda.

Cherry and I discussed contracts and budget. We have much to do. God's plan is before us. We pray for wisdom. We are excited for all that has happened since 2/1/97.

I must call Gary Loster, Mayor in Michigan. He highly suggests Cherry, Celestin, and I go to Nigeria in September. The door is open for us. Who knows what will happen with China. Jeff continues to say things are closing, but it bears no fruit.

Today, Cherry and I received a picture from our Driver Mussa Hussan Ali. He desires to return to school to complete his education in Hotel Management/Catering.

2/20/97 ~ 4:05 a.m.

For the first time in three weeks, I have felt the financial/managerial processes of operating Four-D Success Academy. Cherry said I looked totally relaxed after the 1st week. But at 11:00 p.m. on 2/19/97, I was on the telephone with Pam and Frankie. The finances at the school are grim. The bank denied the $150,000 line of credit. They want me to apply for a small Business Loan. Payroll is due Friday and the accounts, I'm told, have $54. Lord, what will You have me to do? We discuss income, funds, staff, immediate cuts, and projections for the next three months.

I am at a point where I must ask Ernell for $5,000 from our line of credit. The last $8,000 I borrowed I paid back myself, vowing never to request funds from him again. He made it so clear he wanted his money back. It didn't belong to us (never). I have felt alone with Four-D Success Academy for several years.

I've asked the Lord, what am I to do? I have tossed and turned. Unable to think clearly, I cry; there's a flash of pain. I have sent forth my best effort to help others, family, friends, strangers, and now I find another financial crisis which seems to tear my insides apart, and cause my mind to float. Lord, what am I to do?

I must call Peggy @ the bank.

- ✓ Cash in my SAR SEP, Deposit funds to FDSA Account.
- ✓ Cash in IRA, deposit to account.
- ✓ Contact T. Jones regarding Financial Aid Package.
- ✓ Possibly see someone regarding investments in FDS.
- ✓ God, keep me focused, keep Four-D Success Academy alive.

2/20/97 ~ 8:10 a.m.

I started talking with Cherry and never made an entry.

2/21/97 ~ 8:25 a.m.

Cherry and I talked about the financial problems of the school. She immediately began to tell of what she could do: Put money from savings, hold checks (payroll), etc. She is truly my business partner.

It is wonderful to have one who is as interested as I am. I cried, feeling I had put her in a horrible financial crisis. She is considering resigning from the School District due to problems and her work with FDSA. Now with the work through CLS International and working in Rwanda, her choice of employment is hers.

God truly is looking out for Four-D Success Academy. Wednesday night, I had knots in my stomach. For the first time in three weeks, I felt the reminders of pressure related to my responsibilities at home. I had forgotten what it felt like to relax. I will truly miss this place.

Yesterday, we (Celestin, Caritas, Cherry, and I) visited Celestin and Caritas's precious home site. It was solemn. Caritas described the house to us. Only partial walls (3-4) remain. Celestin explained his family was in the house. The second day after the bombing of the Presidents planes, his family home was attacked. His father and brothers were taken from the house, separated and killed. The militia threw grenades into the house, killing his mother, aunt, and anyone else in the house. The house was demolished. The property is large. One can tell it was a beautiful place. Many banana trees, cows — it's a large house.

While visiting people across the street, an old woman walked by. She claimed her sons participated in killing Tutsis. She was proud of them, she boasted that they even took furniture from Caritas home and it was in her home. She had no sorrow or remorse. She walked off talking about not curing, no regrets, she was old, not to live much longer.

I can't imagine how Caritas and Celestin felt at that moment.

Caritas took us to a clinic. Cherry and I were so impressed. It was clean, organized, with limited equipment, but well-managed. The nurses took care of the residents in the area. No M.D. on staff. They diagnosed, treated, delivered babies. Compared to the General

Hospital, the clinic was heaven. The General Hospital was leaning towards hell.

Next we went to the school site and gravesite of their parents and siblings. Cherry and I stayed behind. It was raining hard. Caritas showed Celestin where the graves were marked. His first trip home. I held my tears. He shows nothing. The tightness in his jaw said much. We moved on.

I have truly loved being here. I look forward to my return.

Aisha called me today. She has been the only family member to call me. Ernell did call after she told him I needed money. But other than that, "0 - zip". I assume he gave Pam the loan of $5,000. Tahira thinks I am still with the Ambassador in Ethiopia. Aisha wanted to make sure I was coming home Sunday. I miss them.

Today, we will be busy. Appointments with Alex. Invitation to Jane's restaurant at 1:00. Meeting with Charles at 2:00. Caritas and the Woman's Organization at 6:00. Party at 9:00. Saturday at 12:30 we will be on the plane.

2/22/97 ~ 4:43 p.m.

We're up and away, going home. Yesterday we were treated to lunch at La Elegance, Jane's restaurant. Great food. Alexis gave Cherry a large map of Rwanda. She was beside herself. Last night we danced at the Cadillac. Good company and fun. Earlier we met with Charles for business. He wants us to find a passenger aircraft and equipment for road repair. CLS International is in business.

Alexis delivered a letter to us this morning. It expressed his love of us, welcoming us to his family, and sharing his land. He and Ida dressed up to see us off at the airport, along with Caritas, Alfred,

Kevin, Musafe, Ollie, Celestin, and three ladies from the orphanages. As our plane took off, I looked out the window and I could see Alexis waving.

I look forward to returning home to this beautiful family.

Cherry and I have learned so much about each other, friendship, love, business, cultures, relaxation, and history. I will always cherish the memories. I am so thankful to God for this experience and opportunity. I pray for focus and productivity.

Linda Smith - Umuhoza

2/23/97 ~ 8:00 a.m.

Well, we have arrived in London after flying and stopping all night. Rwanda to Ethiopia to Aswan Uganda, Cairo Egypt to London. Cherry started crying after we received the first meal on Ethiopia Airline from Rwanda. It was horrible. The stewardess asked her what was wrong and she cried, "The food tastes bad, and I miss my friends." I laughed so I would not cry. We talked about the new family we have – their friendship, love, kindness, relationships – and all the good things that have come our way. Now in London we shall locate Helen to deliver goods.

We saw Airline Mauritius. One day we are going to Mauritius.

2/24/97 ~ 12:20 a.m.

The flight out of London was delayed four hours due to electrical problems with the intercom system. We all exited the first plane with bags and totes to wait for another. While eating breakfast in the London Airport, I began to cry. I thought of all the warm, loving, hugs and kind words that were expressed to me by the Rwandans.

How much of what they had, I needed and longed for. Cherry talked about our future, our travels ahead, business, and my life. She sees a different life for me.

Emmanuel was at the LA Airport waiting for us. It was a delight to see a waiting, smiling face. The drive home was filled with laughter, tears, talking, and silence. We miss Rwanda and its people — our new family members.

Upon arriving home, we were greeted by Aisha. When I entered the house, Ernell was sitting in his chair talking on the phone with my brother. He got up, hung up the telephone, and sat in the high chair. I greeted him with a hug. I shared my trip, talked about different sites. I hauled my heavy bags upstairs (Aisha had asked him to bring it up, but he didn't move). I unpacked and talked with Tahira and Aisha.

I showered and washed my hair. Aisha dried and curled it. At 1:10 a.m. she is done and I am tired. I thank God for all I have and have experienced. I look forward to a bright future in working in Rwanda and Internationally. Thank You, Lord for a safe trip.

I call Alex's home and left a message with Ida.

2/24/97 ~ 11:59 p.m.

What a day. Alex called from Rwanda with greetings of good will. We agreed to stay in contact with each other on a weekly basis.

I had a meeting with the staff to discuss the financial situation. Pamela and Frankie had prepared current status: three month projects for my review along with recommendations. The enrollment has been low in all classes. Riverside site has cost us to remain open and we have not had a class there since May '96. I had to lay off

Margie and cut Chris to 20 hours a week. Betty's last day may be Friday until we receive new enrollees, cut Mary to three days week, Nancy to four days a week. Shirley is off on sick leave. She is scheduled for surgery on April 7, 1997. I had a sense of peace. I know I could no longer worry with stomach pains. I had come to relax, pray, and talk with God. He knows my every need. He knows what I have aimed to do. He knows I need Him. I always pray for focus, wisdom, knowledge, and peace. I always pray for guidance.

The school will receive recognition for its achievements from the San Bernardino Private Industry Council. What a nice notice in troubled times. I received a call from Pamela. That's what got me out of bed to write. She was crying. Margie had called to inform her that her mother (Margie's) had died. We all knew her mother was very ill and had been hospitalized for the past year. The loss of her job and the loss of her mother are overwhelming. Pam was crying. I felt empty. What bad timing. I rose to write and pray. I think of all that has happened today. I felt peaceful, yet sorrowful.

Aisha entered the room to inquire about Margie's mother. We discuss Margie's situation, the nursing school financial situation, and Rwanda. She recommended a prayer meeting. I inform her I am always in prayer. I am praying as I sit here thinking and waiting.

It's now 12:35 a.m. I will go before the Lord and kneel and pray. I know He will answer and take care of all things that are for good. Lord, I thank You. For through times like these, it is not my strength that I stand, but Yours.

1:05 a.m.

After prayer, I called Caritas in Rwanda. When she answered the phone, I said, "Hello Mama." She knew it was me. She called Musafe to the phone. He and I talked. He was pleased we had arrived safely. He sends his greetings to Don and Cherry. It was good to feel Rwanda and hear his voice, the expression of the language.

I long to return. He hopes Aisha will make the journey on my next trip.

I spoke with my mother today. She was glad I returned safely. It was nice to hear her express her love for me, indirectly. She has held so much back over the years. It was good. Lord, as I retire, fill me up! Use my hands, Lord, and my feet. Use my heart, Lord. Speak to me. If you can use me, Lord, please use me.

2/27/97 ~ 11:20 p.m.

I returned home. Now I know why I cried so much as I headed towards California. Aisha greeted me at the van. Ernell was on the phone. I think about the joy I felt in Rwanda and the sadness I feel here. I gained peace and tranquility. Some have said I am not the same. I am not. The financial situation has not caused me to panic. I know I have done my very best. I know God has always provided for the school, and He will not close the school doors. I feel peace. I know my future and the future of my child will be guided by God. The work that lies ahead is plentiful.

I write letters to Charles, Caritas, Vincent, and Joseph. They will be faxed in the morning. I am tired and it's time to retire.

Cherry is doing well. She resigned from the School District. God is her guide. He will see us through our current dilemma.

3/4/97 ~ 5:09 p.m.

I sit in my office thinking about the events that have occurred since returning home. I visited my mother and nephews. They were all glad to see me. I shared my pictures and expressed my joy in being in Rwanda. Sadiq, my brother who is incarcerated, called and was delighted that I had returned home safely. I could see his smile. I will travel to see him at the end of the month. I felt absolutely wonderful on Saturday. I woke up at 4:30 a.m. and rose by 5:15, went into my kitchen, and began cleaning out my refrigerator. By 5:45, I was washing clothes. I cleaned bathrooms and went grocery shopping by 2:30. I decided to rent movies. I was alone at home. My chores complete. The house was mine until 3:00 p.m. Ernell returned home from his ski trip. But that didn't interfere with my tranquility. I even cooked dinner! Sunday was a blessed day at Church. Pastor Chuck taught on *Victim – Victor … Never Give Up on a Dream*. I felt as though he was having a personal conversation with me. God continues to reaffirm His presence in my life. Monday 3/3, Cherry and I represented CLS International in a meeting with engineers. We are seeking to bring Charles and this group together for business.

I sung *Lead Me* all the way to school. The Lord knows all. I need peace, financial peace. I feel calm, pleasantly calm.

Roberta (JTPA) called to say a $7,000 check was in the mail. God delivers. A young man named Mr. Johnson from Wells Fargo called. We discussed loans. He is mailing me an application. He told me to return it to him personally. I'm seeking $20,000-$30,000 thousand. I know God will enable me to pay off the loans. A representative from KGGI, Cory, called today to discuss advertising on the radio. He is willing to help Four-D Success with marketing. Well, he called back to inform me he had received the okay for airtime. 60-minute interview, 40 printed questions. This is great!

Last Friday, Steve Pakin from the Riverside Press Enterprise came to Graduation with a photographer. Steve had interviewed me on Thursday. I wasn't sure if he would print/write the story or not, but he returned on Friday. I am looking forward to his article.

The SB PIC nominated Four-D Success for the outstanding training we provide to the San Bernardino County residents. What an honor!

Two weeks ago, we had $57.00 in the account with payroll due. We are still here! FAITH NEVER FAILS ME! GOD IS GOOD ALL THE TIME. God knows I have done my best. I rely on God to make a way for us. He will. The foundation on which we stand is good and for God.

LORD, THANK YOU FOR MY PERSONAL BLESSING.

I'M HERE!

3/5/97 ~ 5:45

I had a need to pray with the staff today. I reminded them that we must pray to God when times are tough. There is a lot going on with the school and staff in their personal lives. We prayed for the school, for each person in the circle, Frankie and husband Bill, Adenia, Crissandra's ill son, home, Pam and home, me and home. We prayed for Shirley's knees, Betty's finances, and Cherry's personal situation. God answers prayers.

Community Bank of California denied the request for the loan. I was referred to three other sources. I did receive a return call from Nick Landers with EDC. He listened, said he would make some calls to help. God, guide him. Each day, things get tight. I pray to remain calm. I pray for a positive financial aid report.

I am trying my best!

3/13/97 ~ 12:34 a.m.

Well, what has happened this past week?

I called 8-10 different individuals seeking funding for the school – even the President of Business Bank of California. Everyone referred me to someone else. By the time I met with the rep from Citizens Bank, I was told I couldn't show a profit, that I was losing money, and that she wasn't sure she could help me. I told her she was the last person I was going to ask for help. If I could show a profit, I wouldn't be sitting with her then. By the time someone would say they can provide assistance, I wouldn't need any. I was not going to fail or go out of business. God is going to see us through. I felt convinced and calm. Enough was enough. God knows what I am about. He knows what Four-D Success Academy is about. He is my banker.

The students are coming in for Monday's class, 20 are enrolled. From $10,000-$80,000. A marketing rep from KGGI (99.1) named Cory came by last week to seek business. All I could do was laugh and tell him I had no money to advertise. Now, if he wanted to help, fine. He returned to his office and called with the offer to present me on 99.1 on the Sunday show as their featured guest (6-7 a.m.) Today we pre-recorded with Shannon Casey. One whole hour to talk about Four-D Success Academy. Shannon said she might air it twice!

The article came out in the Press Enterprise yesterday. It was good. It gave me the courage I sought for the school.

Linda L. Smith

We were going to drop all efforts to bring the Ambassador to California. Then he called Cherry and said he would come at our request! Well, the planning is back on! A small focused group of us will work together to bring this about with God's help!

Cherry, Frankie, and I have worked on the budget for Rwanda. It's coming along. I spoke with Dr. Vincent Biruta in Washington on the 8th? He indicated they were waiting for the proposal. That's a great sign. The road proposal in Rwanda is $50 million, if/when the engineers accept the offer to do the work, and we could earn a hefty commission.

I spoke with Gary Loster, Mayor of Saginaw, Michigan. He and I discussed a Nigeria trip for September. He is going on the 15th of March and has requested a package from us to present to the Minister of Health. He is providing the way, as Joseph Mutaboba did for Rwanda.

Tonight, Aisha's boyfriend Jared told me he was proud of me. All I could do was hug him! He meant it.

Lord, thank You.

I took a copy of the article to my mother. She was delighted and said she had to give it to a member of her Church to read. It felt good to receive her acknowledgment. The child in me was happy!

Heavenly Father, I thank You for my peace. For FDSA, for keeping us open.

Oh yes — I received a call today from Mr. Greer who works with Pacific Travel Trade School. His boss, Ms. Diana Green, has offered the full use of her facilities in Long Beach for us to teach the DSD class. I will meet with her staff next week. God is good. I am tired.

Tomorrow I meet with T. Jones — Financial Assistant. I expect good things. Goodnight, Lord.

Your Child, Linda

3/15/97 ~ 11:15 a.m.

If God ever wanted me to know His presence in Four-D Success Academy, Inc., it was revealed to me yesterday at the Graduation. The seven of the original students who had started with Shirley in January had called themselves the "Magnificent Seven." Their goal was to achieve academic excellence. They did. All seven students earned an A+ throughout the program. Four of the seven had perfect attendance, and one student read Maya Angelou "Still I Rise." I am always drawn to tears at a graduation, but this was more. I love what I do. I am so blessed to have the opportunity to make a difference in their lives. I will continue to give all I can.

Frankie, Pam, and I met with Tonya Parker Jones and a lady named Donna from Eldorado Consultant Services to discuss our Financial Aid Program. We are targeting to start the program up in April. This will be a milestone for us. Financially, we should become much more stable.

The CLS Consultants made positive contact with an emergency firm in LA. The reconstruction of roads in Rwanda is looking good.

Aisha Smith, my daughter, was hired yesterday by Pam and Frankie to work as a clerk in the office. We now have an ally in the Riverside Office. Kathy attended the Graduation. We talked about FDSA in Riverside and what we need to do to hold a class. I thank God for her support.

I can't be anything but glad that I know the Lord!

Linda L. Smith

3/16/97 ~ 10:15 p.m.

Aisha and I attended the 11:00 a.m. service at Loveland, known as LL Prime Time. Focus is on the youth and contemporary music.

Pastor Chuck and I spoke briefly after Church Services. He said I would receive a call from the Love Notes Editor for a featured story. The interview that was pre-recorded Thursday aired today. I am pleased with it. I know God is with us. Tomorrow, Cherry and I will meet with the engineer firm about roads for Rwanda.

God is good.

3/17/97 ~ 9:30 a.m.

I sit here listening to Gospel. They are singing, *"If you are having problems, try Jesus. Jesus knows what you are going through, He's right there beside you."*

Today, 23 students enrolled into the CNA class. Jesus takes care of us. God is able. When all the financial entities told me no, I was losing money and they couldn't/wouldn't help, I tried Jesus. I knew He knew what I/we needed and what our future held. Today, Jesus brought us $92,000.

3/20/97 ~ 5:20 p.m.

I know we are coming out of the Valley. I spoke with Keith last night. I was informed about the funds that are available for training. He recommended I speak with Betty Woods, which I did today. We discussed the possibility of us doing Intake. We will discuss it further next week. I requested 30 students for 4/7/97. I visited Long Beach Trade School for possible training site for DSD. Looks good.

The school needs to be on the Internet. I placed a call to Dr. Lassiter for help.

242

The Ambassador, Theogene Rudasingwa, is coming April 25th-28th. We are planning for his visit. I feel quite sleepy and tired. I have much to do. I will retire early, rise early, and come into the office.

We have a balance of $13,497.28. Payroll is tomorrow. There are dollars available on the Wells Fargo Business Card of $9,000. God is good. He continues to supply our needs!

Love You.

3/31/97 ~ 8:25

"Be encouraged." Those were Robert Rochelle's words to me this morning. I know God is real, and He lights the path I travel. There are times I know Satan attacks. I worry about finances. I sought help. I finally became tired of individuals telling me I was losing money. That's why they couldn't help!

4/1/97 ~ 7:19 a.m.

I did not finish from yesterday. I know that God leads Four-D Success Academy. I know He will show me the way to go. Be encouraged. I asked the manager in Riverside to allow the rent to stay at $2,500 a month. He hasn't responded, so I will take that as a yes!

Cherry and I are working with several other ladies to plan for the Ambassador's visit. We will hold the function at the Academy on 4/24/97. I am so looking forward to it. I haven't heard from the Department of Education about our Financial Aid, but I did receive a bill for $3,000 from El Dorado College. I know it was worth it, although I did most of the work on my computer. We have students lined up to go. We continue to act on faith. How else can we proceed?

Frankie's sister was in a car accident. I am praying for a speedy recovery for her and her children.

San Bernardino County JTPA Media Department came to the office today to interview Cherry and I. They took pictures of the LVN students in action for the Recognition Dinner on 4/25/97 as an outstanding service provider for students.

I've joined a committee to receive Maya Angelou on 5/10/97 at the Phenix Book Store. This will be a privilege and exciting. I hear a cricket in my house. My grandmother said that meant funds are coming! Payday is Friday. Lord, do Your thing! We must stay focused on God's mission for us – to help make a difference in someone's life.

Yesterday, Cherry shared with me Dr. Vincent Biruta is now Minister of Health and he wants our proposal. Charles and Celestin want to come to meet with J Best Engineering about the proposal in Rwanda. Things seem positive.

Diana Green with Pacific Trade School offered her facility for training on Saturday, and possibly 10 weeks for a CNA program in LA. Diana desires to work together regarding a LVN Program. Not bad for a day.

Thank You, Lord for Your blessings. Love, Your Child

Oh yes, Sadiq called me. I will be seeing him on Friday 4/11/97.

4/3/97 ~ 10:50 p.m.

Today, God was here! Payday is tomorrow. There is $13,000 in the account. Nancy offered to hold her check and two others didn't turn in acceptable time sheets. Cherry and I will not cash our checks until Monday. God will cover those that are cashed.

Today Bob Smith, referred by Charlie, came by to provide information on financing (buying receivables). Bob and I will meet Friday evening at the office to discuss possibilities. We are still waiting to hear from US Ed about Financial Aid. Monday, CNA classes start. There are nine in Colton and four in Riverside. I pray for more, like 15 students each.

Next week, I visit my brother Sadiq. We have much to share about. Most important will be discussing his sons.

Goodnight!

4/4/97 ~ 11:05 p.m.

We are an Accredited Vocational Nursing Program! Today, Cherry and I flew to Oakland, CA, for the Quarterly LVN/Psychiatric Board Meeting.

We were approved to start an April class with 30 students, and our consultant's report recommended the accreditation.

I've yet to savor the full impact of being the President/Founder of the only African-American Accredited Vocational Nursing School and Vocational Program. Cherry is the first African-American Director and Developer of an LVN curriculum approved by the State. We are good at what we do. God has blessed us to venture forward and blaze a new path. The reality is I have never viewed myself as someone capable of running such a successful business. I never thought of myself as "SMART," only consistent in my endeavors, sitting on a plan and asking God to guide me. Yet I am humbled by our accomplishments. I guess that's why I haven't given much thought to what I have personally achieved. I feel that what I have done has been through God's grace. He gave me the vision and He alone can take it away. I continue to be thankful to God for having the opportunity to give to others and to help make a positive difference in their lives.

I don't know where God will take Cherry, Four-D Success Academy, Inc., and me next, but we are ready for the work and ride. I view Cherry as a partner, not an employee. God sent me a wonderful gift.

4/14/97 ~ 6:30 p.m.

I traveled to Sacramento to visit Sadiq, but due to the escape of an inmate, all visiting was put on hold. I did have the opportunity to attend a workshop on Charter Schools. I met Palel and Valarie White. They are associated with Bellevue Santa Fe Charter School in San Luis Obispo, CA.

Today I feel awfully low. I get like this every two weeks. There's $4,400 in the checking account, bills as usual and payroll due Friday. I received a call from Percy Harper (Pastor). He spoke to my spirit, my needs, my prayer, without me saying a word. God has taken me to a point of "brokenness." I know I need Him. It is He, not I. I truly needed and appreciated Percy's words and prayer. There are times I forget how blessed me/FDSA am, and that God has continued to cover us. He never told me how He was going to do it – He just gave me my assignment. I stop and reflect a moment on that statement. I am in the co-pilot seat. He is the pilot.

I received a call from Elyda, JTPA. I forgot/missed a page requesting my signature for payment. The total $12,000. I walked over, signed, and requested. I hand carried the payment voucher to Mr. Lee's office. I ask Veronica to obtain his signature today and pass the form on to Roberta, "My Angel of Mercy." She will put a rush on it. Payment will be received by Monday.

Kathy Grusso informed me she is working to enroll Sara Bolder into the program for LVN. She has also requested to be assigned to us as our liaison. This is good for us!

I spoke with Eileen Pace with enrollment info, a seven-week CNA program in LA. I have scheduled the space and received approval for clinical training at Good Samaritan Hospital. Enid Hamilton is scheduled to teach the class.

Aisha is on the move for a new truck. Once she has an ideal, she succeeds. Lord, keep my feet planted on solid ground.

Let me hear You and follow without question or doubt!

Let me state what I claim, and claim all You have stated for me.

Help me to organize myself and each team member.

4/16/97 ~ 11:05 p.m.

Well, tomorrow we will hear the outcome of our application to Fed Financial Aid Program. God has sustained us thus far. This has been a long wait. God is good. Jeff Carrillo, Chairman of Advisory Board, advised me not to sign up for financial assistance through Finance Co. I shall follow his advice. God, guide me.

4/19/97 ~ 7:45 a.m.

Well, the Fed Express delivery never arrived. We don't know the outcome of the financial aid application. Part of me knows it's okay and that God has it all under control. I guess that's why I feel calm. I haven't called Bob Smith back with the financing program, Ed Carrillo advised against it. I'll notify him on Monday.

We are doing fine at the school. Some personal issues have been addressed. Shirley is scheduled for surgery Monday. Knees are bad. I have been working hard with Cherry on the reception for Theogene Rudasinga, Ambassador from Rwanda. We will have a reception at Four-D Success Academy.

I received a call from Wayne Bradley, a young man who attended the graduation of the "Magnificent 7" – Adenia/Shirley March '97 Class. He witnessed the graduation, our sincerity to our students. He will be speaking with the Mayor of Compton Omar Bradley, his brother, about the school's training program. We briefly discussed my attempts over the past 4 years to enter into Compton. He understands the politics of the City. I should receive a call within 7 days for an appointment.

Enid Hamilton and I met with Jo Romon at Good Samaritan Hospital. We will be holding a class there starting May 5th. I expect success. Eileen is working diligently on enrolling students. My friend was admitted into the hospital last evening. Ruth is weak, having fainting spells. She is positive about her outcome – one way or another. Her brother, Charles, has watched over her with great care and love. I pray for them both.

I sat here thinking about the LVN students and began to cry. I pray and thank God for all we have been through. Cherry and I have worked diligently on this program. We have cried and struggled, but the outcome is this: students will graduate, pass their boards, and become LVN's. I cry thinking of all the possibilities now open to them.

God is good.

I pray to Him for guidance, support to increase my capabilities, and growth (personally). I pray that He is satisfied with me. That FDSA is an area in my life that I am truly dedicated and true. Lord, I do love You and what You have given me.

4/21/97 ~ 10:12 a.m.

Yesterday was an emotional day for me. Lots of crying, I feel overwhelmed with Ernell. No communication, as though I am afraid to ask him things for fear of the nonchalant rejection he may give. I keep hearing his response to my questions, "How was your trip?" His response was filled with excitement and enthusiasm, "It was great." No more. No less. No discussion. I no longer desire to be here. I fear God would punish me for wanting to leave. Is my punishment not hearing the results of the Financial Aid outcome? I went to Cherry's house crying after Church at 8:00 p.m. She explained that God isn't going to punish her. She works for the Academy; surely He would put me in a position to continue to help others.

My confusion is real to me. My sadness is real. I have felt so lonely over the years. No conversations worth a dime. A man who can live in solitude. As long as I am here to be seen, that seems enough for him. But I don't think he really sees me. He never compliments me or any changes about me, my work, and my desires. The house (when I did do daily cleaning). Who am I to him? I don't know.

I must turn in the SB Co. contract today. The city of SB contract has been approved.

Lord, guide me – help me though the storm. I feel I will be taking care of Anwar and Jaise in the near future.

Lord, give me the place to raise them.

Linda L. Smith

4/21/97 ~ 10:35 p.m.

Well, if I cry, I can't think. The report was not as we prayed for. We were denied into the Federal Financial Aid Program. Tonya did not call to tell me. I had to call her. The form seems to be dated 4/11/97.

I will call U.S Ed in the morning for clarification. As Perry, Eldorado's controller, talked with me about options and explains the financial statement as he saw it, I realized my report had not been reviewed prior to submission! I waited four months on something quite presentable — a denial.

Cherry and I talked. She is truly a trooper, and we discussed our options.

I called Jimmy, explained the situation and requested $20,000-$25,000. I will call him in the morning before noon with an exact amount. We may be able to show positive cash flow, resubmit, and allow an approval. I have organized my thoughts. I pray as I write: God, keep me focused, and without fear.

Eileen called to report she had 10 students, good chance for 15. That's $60,000 for June. We must prevail and hold on. If God be with us, who can be against us?

Thank You, Jesus.

The reception for the Ambassador is going ahead as planned. We expect a great time.

4/23/97 ~ 7:40 a.m.

Yesterday, I was at Greg Sheet's office by 8 a.m., waiting for him to discuss the outcome of the denial letter. I guess I should go back, because I was up at 4:45 thinking when I should call the Washington Department of Education. At 5:30, I had Tracy on the line. She referred me to Robert Smith, the Financial Analyst. He and I discussed the financials; I have to have Greg call him. I spoke with Chris in San Francisco, the Consultant in Region 9. He was not able to answer any of my questions!

I spoke with Jimmy. I was seeking financial support. Jimmy may be able to assist. I submitted an application to Wells Fargo to move the Line of Credit into a Prime loan. I request Bank of America do the same. I will know in 2-3 days. I submitted the financial statement to San Bernardino County Small Business Enhancement Program. John will reveal to me if it is possible for funding ($25,000). Frankie and I reviewed the financials and looked at what adjustments could be made. She will work at home for the next two days.

T. Jones took the call I placed to the President of the company. I let her know I was totally frustrated. It was evident that the financial report of the Academy was not reviewed. She tried to say I was out of the Country. I reminded her the application was received in her office on 1/24/97. I left on 2/5/97 — the same day she mailed the application.

I cried a lot after everyone had gone home. Tonya and the students left at 8:30. God, I know I have tried. I am not quitting, but weary. I pray and ask that He renew my strength and focus.

I woke up this morning feeling refreshed; last night, I wrote out plans to realign staff. We will make it. God is good.

I opened a paper today and read, "All things are possible through God." We will make it. Love You, God, and Four-D Success Academy.

4/24/97 ~ 11:45 p.m.

Exhausted, but I can't go to sleep before I write about this wonderful day and yesterday.

The Ambassador, Dr. Theogene Rudasinga His Excellency of the Republic, of Rwanda arrived at 7:05 p.m. at Ontario Airport on 4/23/97. Dr. Don Bell, Cherry, and I received him in his room at the Red Lion Inn Hotel in Ontario. What a delight. We discussed the agenda, went out to dinner, and then retired back to his room for further discussion. I arrived home tired and excited at 11:03 p.m.

Today, I picked up Cherry and we met the Ambassador and Al Barnum at the hotel. We had a full schedule. Edison in Irwindale was to meet Bell Thomas and Greg Sharp for a tour. Dr. Rudasingwa had the opportunity to drive the battery-operated car. He had fun with this and pictures were taken. Then we were off to Loma Linda to Emmanuel and Jean's home for lunch. The meal was planta, potatoes, chicken, and vegetables. The serving style brought me back to Rwanda. Emmanuel began to speak about the joy of God, the laughter and goodness of God. Everything would be all right. I had to go to the bathroom to cry. God had sent His messenger to me. Everything was okay. We left there and went to the International Public Health Department and met Emmanuel's boss Dr. Hart. Next we went to meet Dr. Joan Coggin, a delightful lady who presented us with LVN Key rings. From there we had a tour of the Medical Center. Neonatal ICU Cardiac Unit, an opportunity to see a nine-day-old baby who was a twin. She was negative one pound at birth. The twin died soon after birth. The doctor was going to let her go. He took her off the respirators and she continued to breathe.

We met Dr. Bailey, the noted surgeon for Baby Joy, the infant who received a baboon's heart and died 21 days later. New technology. I learned something today. Now to Four-D Success Academy for the reception. What a turnout. The food was great and close to 200 people came. The Ambassador was very pleased with the reception. With God's help, we were successful. We were assisted by the Black Nurses Association, the Inland Chapter of NCNW. The Ambassador was interviewed by The Sun, Black Voices, and a TV interview with Channel 3. He is scheduled for LA Times and the Precinct Reporter. He was presented acknowledgments from Assemblyman Joe Boca, (Michael Townsend), Police Chief Dennis Hegwood, Colton Councilwoman Betty Cook NCNW, Beverly Powell, Edison, and Dr. Don Bell. Many pictures were taken. Cherry was interviewed by Channel 3 as well.

What a blessing this day has been. My feet are tired but I am full of joy. Tomorrow is a new day and a busy one. 7:15 a.m. in Ontario to Cal Poly, an evening at the Red Lion for an award. God is good. God is good.

Thank You, Lord.

4/28/97 ~ 10:55 p.m.

I've been so busy that I have not written a thing about the excitement over the last five days with the Ambassador Theogene Rudasinga, His Excellency, the Embassy of the Republic of Rwanda visit.

Well, Cherry and I picked Theogene up at the Ontario Airport at 7:05 p.m. on 4/23. Well, on Friday we started out with Al Barnum at 7:15 a.m. We arrived at Cal Poly to visit the English Institute where Claire is a student. Then Theogene, Don Bell, Cherry, and I visited High School students on the International High School. The

Ambassador had all eyes and ears fixed on him. Katherine was in Class. I know she was too proud of her mom! From there, the Ambassador visited college students and faculty. At noon, we had the lunch with the Deans and met the University's President. By 4:00, we were ready to return to the hotel. At 6:00 we were on our way to the Red Lion to receive the Ambassador, and to attend the award dinner in which FDSA was being recognized as 1 of 3 outstanding schools in the Inland Empire area. I had to stop and write a letter to Dr. Height.

The Ambassador spoke to the attendees. He captures the crowd! I spoke and received accolades. It truly was a wonderful evening.

On Saturday, he and I (Al Barnum) went to a meeting in LA at the Monitor Institute there we met Pippa Scott, Anna and Judge Bruce. We discussed digitalizing film to record the history of Rwanda Genocide.

I will follow up along with Cherry on new assignments. To Cal Poly for Cultural Exchange and Gospel Proposal. We are tired but it was great. 70-80 people, great food, wonderful weather, atmosphere. Everything was great!

After the guests were gone, Cherry, Don, Emmanuel, and Theogene met to wrap things up. He gave us an assignment. Ways to improve communication among team and focus on goals. All was well-received.

Sunday we attended Church of Christ in Perris for service and a program. At 1:30, off to Van Nuys for a meeting with ITT and Dimensions Inc. to discuss Radar Tech. Met Bob and Burk – great brothers. Theogene bid us goodbye. We left him at The Hilton with

Emmanuel. Cherry and I hit the road home, talking all the way about the five exciting days we had just experienced.

Monday, I am working on how to get the Financial Aid Program going. Final solution and options. Increase student enrollment, increase revenue, and decrease cost of operation. Conference call with Greg Sheets, Cherry, and Frankie, and we will work on it.

Received Individual Referral from SB Co. to train IV Therapy, Acute Nurse Aide and Phlebotomy Class to current students. This will help.

Friday, Enid and I go to LA for Pacific Asian Consortium in Employee (PACE) – Orientation of students.

I assess my output and home money. I request to delete the cable for three months. Ernell won't hear of it. He is not willing to sacrifice his TV to help.

This shall be over soon; I am tired I have much to do other than concern myself over this TV. He couldn't even focus on me yesterday while I was trying to share the excitement of the Radar program with him. TV is too much competition for me. He can have it.

Lord, thank You for my peace within. I know we will make it, only You know how.

5/1/97 ~ 9:05 p.m.

On 4/29/97, we received the fax from Dr. Vincent Biruta. They are interested in our proposal. Cherry and I spoke at 11:00 p.m. What excitement. We don't know what or when we'll all be going. A 5-year contract! She drafted a letter, called me back at 12:30 a.m. We discussed it! 25 were faxed. We are now awaiting the response. I am trying to find a way to address the financial plight of the school. I have hit high walls everywhere I travel. I cry out loud today. Cried to God, Why am I suffering like this? I have given all I can to help others. Now You help me. You see me, help me.

I met with Greg Sheets CPA. We discussed Capital Contributions, a revenue, how to increase assets and decrease liability. I spoke with my mom about a loan. I will work on this to assist the school.

I feel drained, yet I must continue to do my best. We have $102,000 outstanding. Payroll is tomorrow with only $10,000 in the account. We owe $20,000 back taxes. Times are tough.

5/3/97 ~ 11:15 p.m.

Life is full of twists. As I struggle with the financial issues of FDSA and decrease income of my own, it seems my husband has plenty. He has felt I have been 'holding out' on him when I had to pay $64,000 in taxes. Once I informed him that money was put into the Corporation on Conversion, his response was, "I paid mine." Well it appears he deposited $2,300 or so into the general account, but kept over $9,000 for himself. I don't feel angry but strained. I sit and write out our bills and mail them.

Cherry and I discuss her next trip to Rwanda. We have planning to do. Aisha and I went out to dinner at the Olive Garden. It's good to be with her. I feel very tired. I must rise at 6:00 for the 7:30 service.

God, I am sorry, I'll try to listen more carefully to You.

On 5/2/97, Friday night, the first LVN students graduated (13 ladies), and Ms. Thelma Bledsoe was the guest speaker. It was a moving ceremony. Cherry presented "The Walter Russ Sr. Scholarship" Guard to Brenda Bolton. God, what an honor to him and me. I talked with my mom about my plight, and she has agreed to help.

If it were easy — everyone would be doing it.

God, thank You.

5/14/97

I haven't taken the time to write for some time. I guess I've felt so overwhelmed, all I could write about would reflect a sense of hopelessness that I know to be false. I still seek financial support for the school.

We received a letter from Dr. Biruta acknowledging the proposal and requesting clarification. We responded within 48 hours. Today, we received another fax asking us to respond to budget forms submitted with focus on Nurse Training with the Dental Clinic.

Cherry and I are quite happy about this. We feel we can effectively manage this 5-year project. I do look forward to the future. I am joyful, yet overwhelmed.

Guide us, Lord.

5/18/97 ~ 8:20 a.m.

It is difficult at times to have a totally joyful day when the home life is unpleasant. Life can certainly become strange. How have I lived so long with a man who cannot consistently express any sense of deep affection? His hugs, I call insignificant embraces, and his kisses have no expression of love. I have expressed my concerns over the years of his insignificant acts, his need to distance himself. I remember coming home and after dinner I put on my robe. He was sitting on the couch. I sat next to him, and then stretched out on the couch with my head in his lap. Within two minutes, he got up, left the room, and returned to sit in his chair. All the while ignoring me, he watched TV in comfort and I guess in peace. I left the room without a word. I know our life together is ending. I simply don't know when.

I know he is preparing. He has several checking accounts. Last month, his check was $9,333 and he placed $2,000 in our account. Only enough to pay the rent. After I refused to pay for anything, he deposited $2,900 more. I do seek a different life for myself. I need not to be with a man who doesn't even care if his daughter attends college, and does not offer a penny towards tuition.

It must (can) be better on the other side.

Frankie and I continue to work diligently toward balancing the account. God, guide us. Through it all, God is LOVE, and I will be okay.

5/18/97 ~ 10:00 p.m.

I had an argument with Ernell. He is too much. When I asked him if he's holding out on money, he smirked a grin and said he's doing what I did. Although I had $64,000 in taxes to pay (without his assistance). I am mad (pissed) after holding so much in. This man doesn't have a clue about love, marriage, openness, or passion. He denies everything. Now I am far from perfect, but I guess my pain, tears, screaming in silence occurred so long ago for such a long period of time that I separated from him long before today.

My fear, as so many other females have, was, "What am I going to do?" How can/will I make it? I had to step through this hold of fear. I do and can and will work to care for me and my children. I must hold on. God will guide Four-D Success and me through the difficult times.

Lord – Today I hear, "Be encouraged." I am.

5/19/97 ~ 11:00 p.m.

Today I feel relieved. God has allowed me to go through the storm and feel peace. Today, 17 CNA's started in Colton and five CNA's started in Riverside. Enid is very disappointed in the students in LA. High absences and low performances. I desire a home for the future. My mother and nephews will one day live with me. God, I know I want to be prepared to receive them well.

I am appreciative for my daughters. Their love, support, spiritual support, and prayers. I want things for my daughters to be well in their lives. I ask God to enable me and FDSA the ability to raise and earn money for their Education. Thank You, Lord.

5/24/97 ~ 7:15 a.m.

Yesterday, 21 CNA students graduated from Adenia's Class. She has another 11, which started on Monday. God continues to bless u. He pays our bills and gives us a salary.

Although my personal life is going through a transition, I know God will see me through as He has seen me through my business life. I pray a home of spirit and joy, love, communication, and laughter, a home of calm and internal peace. A home for my mother, nephews, and children. I know God will guide me.

I am so thankful for the path of FDSA. God has allowed us to touch so many lives in so many ways. I know we may never know the depth we have touched, but the staff and I know we have touched many lives.

Linda L. Smith

The Rwanda Education Project is progressing well. Cherry has truly stepped up the pace. The books are going to be shipped to Rwanda this summer. We are starting to write the proposal for the Education/Training and Dental Program. We are looking at Grants. There is much for us to do. God will send us what we need.

Peace is coming into my personal life. I have made the decision to not live the next 20-40 years in an environment that will produce bitterness in my spirit. Last Sunday, I cried with pain for I know it is time to move on. My daughters are dear to me. I have watched them grow into beautiful young ladies. Each with a distinctive personality and love for life. I am grateful to God that they are close to each other and supportive of each other. I know they squabble over nonsense but siblings do those things. Aisha has truly blossomed; she joined the Church, attends Step class and youth group, and is looking forward to the youth conference.

Tahira is in the last term of her nursing program. She will graduate August 23, '97. What a joy this will be for me. Lord, I thank You for ALL you have given me.

Thank You for my parents who made me. I love them both.

Love Your Child, Linda

5/26/97 ~ 5:55 p.m.

Today is Memorial Day…

I returned to write at 6:50 a.m. on 5/28/97. Memorial Day was quiet for me. We barbequed a nice meal. I overate, slept. Finally, in the late afternoon, Aisha took me walking at the Claremont College. I walked 2 miles and felt great. I think about many things. Yesterday while in the bathroom I thought about my parents and their life – how they didn't communicate throughout their lives together. They never divorced but they were never together. How lonely they must have been. I choose not to repeat their life. Yesterday, I visited an attorney to discuss my situation. I pray for a peaceful departure. The school, I pray and believe will be protected, and guided by God. He gave it to me and only He will take it away. I pray for wisdom, knowledge. Lord, guide me.

5/31/97 ~ 8:15 a.m.

God came through again yesterday. After signing payroll Frankie said, "Well we can cover about three checks." Payroll was $17,000. All I could do was say, "Lord – Bills." I did get a little tense, but I knew all was beyond my control. I was totally reliant upon God.

Driving home Wednesday night, I cried and sang *Lead Me* and *Amazing Grace*. I scream out to God to help me. I know my future is going to change. My marriage has come to an end. Four-D will go on.

I sit still and look back at my life and sometimes cry. I look towards the future and wonder what will be, but I know God has already laid the foundation. I simply must follow the path, accepting all that He has me to do. Maintain the Vision and Purpose. Remember the night He talked to me. Remember the Presence of His power. Through God, ALL things are possible. Four-D Success Academy is proof of that. My mom is helping me. She has agreed to loan me the money, up to $50,000 to address the debt of the Academy. Who would have known of her goodness to me? She still turns from my hugs, my kisses, but I know she cares and loves me. Like Daddy use to say, "She's Eula Mae!"

Yesterday, Alex from Rwanda called. He wanted to know when we were coming back. How nice to know someone wants to truly see you. Hopefully, Cherry and I will be able to return this summer. We are requesting the passport and budget from the Dental Clinic. In fact, that is what I am going to get started on. Lord, I love You. Thank You for my trust, faith, and growth in You.

6/4/97 ~ 10:10 p.m.

Overwhelmed with issues in my life, I told the attorney to hold all proceedings. I need to give full attention to FDSA. It is not possible to prepare emotionally for the separation. As I write, it it's hard to believe. Where did we lose it? At 44, my life is changing. I don't know what God has in store for me. I pray for guidance. I know Ernell will not change, I desire more human contact than he wishes to provide. I have been very lonely in this marriage. Our time alone is silent. No conversation about work, God, life, the children...nothing!

Four-D Success Academy continues to forge ahead. God is blessing us. I witnessed to the Choir. It is a blessing to sing praises to the Lord! It's healing. It's good to know God.

Aisha and I started Step Two last Sunday. She is a blessing; Tahira is excited about Graduation in August. I am pleased with the girls.

6/6/97 ~ 7:00 p.m.

I called T. Jones to apologize about my tone and change in character. The denial for Financial Aid, as I know she did her very best.

I arrived at the office at 6:20 a.m. to find the windows sprayed with the words NIGGERS SUCK KKK. As I pulled my car into the parking stall, I noticed the front door and the window to the right. They appeared to have been marked. As I studied all the windows, I was stunned to read NIGGERS. On the front entrance to the Medical Society, the words NIGGER GO HOME. On the side by the Academy entrance, the words NIGGERS KKK.

I called the Precinct Reporter, the Inland Valley News, the Sun Telegram, and the Police Department. Messages were left at the paper. The police will come to take a report. I called Cris and asked her to bring a camera and film for pictures. I walked around the building. The two-story next to the Academy was sprayed. The front of the Med Society building seemed to have been sprayed, but the windows appeared to have been wiped clean.

I call and left a message on Cherry's recorder. I called the building manager and informed her of the situation. What manner of person would do this? I feel my eyes tearing but I stop. God will see us through this. I will only work harder to follow my assignment from Him. Four-D Success Academy will go in spite of this negative, calculated effort to discourage the staff and me.

7:40 a.m.

Colton Police officer Bornsheuer came to take a report. He asked about disgruntled students. The report will be filed under Hate Crime and will be available in 10 days. Officer Bornsheuer states the tennis shoe print was from a male. At 9:35 a.m. I placed a call to The Black Voice News to report what has happened. The gentleman cleaning the windows, Andrew, states he arrived between 1-2 a.m., removed the words KKK – NIGGER DIE from in front of building door.

Received a call from Jessie James at the NAACP, he will fax a form to fill out. David Perry is here to take pictures for the Inland Valley News Paper. Cheryl Brown, from The Black Voice News, here to take pictures and discuss the need to publish Hate Crimes account.

The building manager is concerned with negative publicity against an associate with the Medical Society building. She states, "I wish it could be swept under the rug." I told her that it could not be put under the rug. The Hate Crime happened, and as a black woman, this is real. Society must be kept aware of these ugly accounts against society.

Cris and I made a presentation to the Riverside site JTPA caseworkers. We received positive comments from several caseworkers. Several state they know we have a very good program. They highly suggest that their clients come to FDSA. We received $16,000 today, deposited $13,000 yesterday, and $14,000 on Friday 5/31. I spoke with Eileen in LA who says $20,000 is coming next week. We strive to meet the 6/30 deadline to have a 1-to-1 ratio plus a positive and gain.

I am tired but not weary. I will continue to put forth my best effort. I looked at my dad's picture. He is smiling. All will be okay.

Friday is Walter Jr.'s Birthday. He's 43 years old. Aisha is at church; Tahira is out with a friend at a pool hall. She must work in the morning. God will turn her around. She shall attend Church.

God, protect and guide us all.

Love, Linda

6/13/97 ~ 7:59 a.m.

Well no further incident regarding the windows and disappearing words. We have continued forward without missing a beat.

Cherry is diligently working on the book collection for REP. Today, she and others will be packing books at Cal Poly and Dr. Don Bell's House.

Financially, the books are looking better. We met with Eldorado Management to discuss invoices, and the process of school and papers. I publicly apologized for my thoughts and anger towards T. Jones. We moved on. We will reapply in July for Financial Aid approval.

Cherry, Roberta, and I worked on the Rwanda Budget from 6 p.m. – 12 midnight, and it is done. A few more items and the complete proposal will be done.

The Rwanda site is slowly coming along. Very small classes, but we are still there. I pray for a full class by July.

The Colton Site is doing okay. Monday, we will start with at least 10 students.

Aisha Smith, my baby, has gone to her first retreat for young adults. I am so very proud of her. Her spiritual growth and focus is wonderful.

Tahira is forging towards graduation. One more month, and she will be through. How proud I am of them. Lord, I thank You for my children.

My life with Ernell has not changed. I think about life without him and I think about what it has been with him. I see myself at times without him. I think about loneliness with him. I feel this. How different will my life be in the future? God only knows. I feel safe.

6/15/97 ~ 7:13 a.m.

Friday is Aisha's 19th Birthday and today is Father's day. Yesterday I went to Daddy's gravesite with a friend. I cried and prayed. I miss him so. Sometimes my life feels so empty with all that I have to do. I lay aside the joy I desire. I know my lack of joy

265

has a great deal to do with my marriage. I feel isolated with a man with whom I have little interest. It is amazing how important a little affection and conversation is with me. I can't get over the feelings of how I felt, when he got up from the couch as I tried to get next to him by placing my head on his lap to watch T.V. That was a turning point for me. Ernell will never understand how I feel. I believe he is preparing himself financially. He refuses to put more then $2,000-2,300 in the checking account, although he makes $6,000-$9,000 a month, but I am okay with this. I now know that God will guide me through whatever path I walk. Today, Aisha is returning from the youth retreat. I am excited to see her. I know she had a wonderful, blessed time.

My mom continues to be a trooper in aiding my financial needs for the school. She hasn't wasted one moment in providing me with items I need. I truly appreciate and love her for this.

I sat on the grounds of the Church and listened to the birds sing. God is good. I need all that we are learning In Step Two class at this time in my life. That God guides us is my prayer. We have a right, and our heritage is success, love, and the happiness of God's word. Through Jesus Christ the Son of God, we are blessed. I am blessed. I am here!

The Academy is doing fine. The finances are getting better. Students are still coming.

Thank You, Lord.

6/17/97 ~ 7:40 a.m.

My Lord, my Lord, give me peace in my spirit today. My God, my God, give me joy in my soul today. My Lord, my Lord, give me *peace in my spirit today. My God, my God, give me joy in my soul today.*

I sung this song on my way to work today. It is so important that I do not allow anything to interrupt my focus and attack my spirit as I face the challenges of each day. I must not be aggressive towards those who attack, but I must remain in a spiritual, tranquil, and peaceful mode. Once I let negativity into my life, my whole equilibrium becomes altered. Negative energy is spent on the unimportant thoughts, and my positive spirit becomes negative, my focus dims and my output lessens.

My Lord, My Lord, give me peace in my spirit today.

Yesterday, Cherry was quite agitated about a message I left on her recorder about the LVN graduates that need to test. Nancy had left a message on her desk to see me. Cherry was quite vocal about how she felt about both. I found myself trying to explain the situation to her in a subservient way. My energy was focused on the Riverside appt, rent cost, and the fiscal issue with the school. I chose not to engage aggressively in conversation with her.

My meeting with Riverside Management went extremely well. Our rent will be $500 a month, thanks be to God's glory. The financial matters at the school are improving steadily. I am thankful to God that I learned the plan from my Father, Walter Russ, Sr. "Hold your Peace." I know what that means. I will hold onto my peace.

Lord, I thank You, I love You, I need You.

6/22/97 ~ 10:15 p.m.

Oh what a blessed day! Brother Lattimore informed me at the Step Two class, that he had a talk with members of the TLC about the Hate

267

Crime at the Academy. Several members were coming to pray after the 2:15 services. Aisha and I were at the Academy with nine members of the TLC. They prayed for us, the school, prayed out Satan and evil principalities. It was such a blessing to have the oil of Jesus anointed on the door and windows. I am so thankful to God for the warriors He sent to me. We never know who is assigned to intercede, but God always comes on time. I know He is there for me.

Tonight at the 6 p.m. service, the CNA members witnessed. Oh what a blessing. Then two young brothers preached. Chris talked about paying the "cost" of doing God's work. How his Father didn't acknowledge his (Chris) calling to the ministry. His lack of support. I know exactly what he was up against.

How difficult it can be when your loved ones don't support the mission God has given you. I gave words of encouragement that his Father in Heaven, the Lord, gives His approval and he would be blessed a 1,000 fold. I just pray for this ministry and I pray that God will just open him up in a special way to be a disciple for Christ to witness to the young and old. Let the ears of the needy listen to the messages God will send by Him. The second young minister, Charles, talked about the Character of Jesus. We can stay the same and be a witness for God, Jesus Christ. To know Christ is to create change in us. I am so thankful to hear these messages. It is what I need to deal with issues at school and home.

God is talking to me.

Lord, let me be wise enough to listen.

6/26/97 ~ 7:30 a.m.

God has a breakthrough for FDSA. Yesterday, I spoke with Robert Smith in Washington D.C. He gave me advice on requesting an appeal for our Financial Aid Status. I thank God for his willingness to aid us. Yesterday, my mom signed the final paper to help me for $37,000. I don't know what to say except "Thank You, Momma and Jesus." Our finances look much better.

Satan has been prayed against at FDSA. The CNA students are not graduating on 7/3. I will keep them until 7/11/97. They must meet the school standards of excellence.

Keith okayed tuition reimbursement for the school. God is good!

6/27/97 ~ 12:03 p.m.

I just collected a $30,000 loan from a friend (high interest at 10% a month). It is available for deposit to help FDSA meet the 1:1 ratio. Given on trust. I am thankful to God for this help. Momma should be signing the loan papers today for $37,000. This will pay our taxes at $28,000.

Today at school all rooms (4), kitchen, and staff office are used for students. God is good. Pam is frustrated with the crowd, but I told her she was handling the issues and that's what I needed. Solutions. No problems. She continues to grow.

On 6/26/97 @ 5:00 p.m. Aisha had surgery. God brought her through. She cried with joy, no fear, no sorrow, just joy of knowing her sweaty palms would be dry. Dr. Ahn entered in the right rib/lung area and covered the ganglion nerve. She has a chest tube and IV's. I thank the Lord, my God, for these blessings.

Linda L. Smith

6/30/97 ~ 11:20

How precious is life? We never know when our last second is on this earth. Today C. Rodgers son, Rome, died of a stroke. He was 19 years of age. He had recently moved to Chicago to live with his older brother.

To hear Rodgers cry out, "My baby is gone, I didn't even get to say goodbye." Lord each day, each second is not promised to us.

I asked the staff to pray. Cherry, Pam, Kay, Betty, Frank and I gathered in my office. Cherry led the prayer. We know Jesus is with Rodgers and her family. I know that Rome knew Jesus. I have comfort in that.

I pray for the family. I will aid in her travel to Chicago with money.

God, today is not promised.

You have told me that YOU will care for me. Yet I worry with man's support.

I thank You for Aisha's health. You allowed me to have my child after surgery another day.

This is a sad day.

Deposited $11,500 from my credit card and $37,064.73 from loan.

We met the 1:1 ratio for Financial Aid with a profit line of $34,000+.

Where do we go from here?

Lord, guide us.

Looking Back …

- The love of God and His Word are my foundation and sustain me through every season and situation in life.

- A three-combo rule to live by… *'Despise not the days of small things; be kind to all people because you never know when you're entertaining an angel sent by God; and, your financier may not look or talk like you.'* The Lord will indiscriminately place people in your life when you least expect it. Don't disregard those fleeting moments of grace.

- It matters not how accomplished you or the business becomes, for both should always evolve toward greater successes. Avoid resting on achievements for too long; instead, use those mountain high experiences as anchors to get you through the valley moments that are sure to come. For it is what you do in the low moments, those trying times that define who you truly are as a leader of the business. Strive to be the compass that others can follow.

- If you would simply believe! From your ability to believe and have faith in what you believe, you will no doubt experience an expansion in ways and places that you least expect. Be open, for many are the plans in man's heart, but God's purpose prevails.

- It's important to stay connected and engaged with family. Find balance between work, family, and God (not necessarily in that order). Be a part of the milestones that are sure to take place over time.

- I am grateful for friends both near and far. My life has been enriched indeed.

- When crises arise and situations look dim, it helps to know the Father, for He alone has the final say!

- I must be ready to fight the good fight of faith at all times. Nothing will come easy, even if ordained by God!
- I discovered early that I would have to be able to multi-task the assignment I was given by the Lord. It's not always easy, yet I trust the reward will be well worth the fight. I am steadfast in Him always!

- Empowering others through education has brought me such tremendous joy and satisfaction. How grateful I am to be able to serve others in an area that I love with all my heart.

- Tomorrow is not promised to anyone. Take time to enjoy life as best you can. I've learned to work hard and play hard. It's a fine line between the two – finding the balance is key.

- Celebrate Life…it's full of promise!

- Distractions will come in every shape, form, and fashion. It's important to recognize when the enemy is rearing his ugly head. We have the insight to see through his madness when we rely on the light to guide our way.

- If it were easy, everyone would be doing it! There are times I must remind myself I am where God wants me, my experiences represent my faith in Him to see me through. I remain hopeful that what He started in me He will complete.

- Relationships will no doubt become strained as you purpose to do God's will for your life. The important thing is to remain focused on the tasks before you. Time reveals all.

The twist and turns of life can overwhelm you if you allow them to. Fasting and prayer really works. They help to keep you humble before God and man. His divine purpose is being worked out in front of all to see. Your shortcomings, pitfalls, and disappointments will be on display, but if you stay true to your passion, His glory will raise you above the heartaches, above the hurts, above the stress and frustration. His glory will bring you into a place of peace and comfort that no one understands how but you. That's the place we should all strive to be in — a place of peace that surpasses all understanding. You may not know how He's going to work it out — just trust that He will.

Linda L. Smith

About the Author

Linda L. Smith, a Registered Nurse for 35 years, combined her love of Nursing, high standards of health care professionalism, and deep spiritual faith, and founded the first and only African-American owned, fully accredited vocational career college in California licensed to teach Vocational Nursing and other allied health care programs. The institution has been recognized as an Outstanding Business by numerous agencies.

Linda has been featured in *Essence Magazine,* is a contributor to the book *Creating Value through People,* and authored *Business by Faith, Integrating the 4D's of Success Personally and Professionally.* In October 2013 a documentary, *Linda L. Smith, A Profile In Courage,* was released and received the Accolade Award.

She was appointed Vice President Board of Trustees for the Inland Empire Loma Linda Ronald McDonald House and to the California State Assistance Fund for Enterprise, Business and Industrial Development Corporation Board of Directors by Governor Brown's Office.

As Founder of Four-D College and an inspirational speaker, she helps women and men pursue their vision with confidence.

Speaking at Colleges, Universities, Conferences, and other events designed to support those pursuing success, particularly in the Health Care Industry and Entrepreneurship/Business and Leadership, Linda teachers her 4D's of Success Personally and Professionally, imparting valuable information to help those who desire to start up a business, or progress in their current business or career path. She shows them how to overcome challenges and achieve success in business and in life.

Her experiences are soul-stirring, her message is powerful, and her delivery is profound. The way in which she shares her personal story, including struggles and adversity, is both educational and empowering.

Linda L. Smith

To book Linda to speak at your event, contact her at www.lindalsmith.com or linda@lindalsmith.com.

www.ingramcontent.com/pod-product-compliance
Lightning Source LLC
Chambersburg PA
CBHW060335200326

41519CB00011BA/1948